Charlie's Secret: Inspired by a True Story

C. L. Heckman

To my husband for “saving” me,

and to our beautiful daughters.

Prologue

"Charlie, wait up!"

I catch a glimpse of my brother jumping a fallen tree while we race to the pond. Branches blow by my face as the spring sun fights to break through the canopy of leaves above. Wiping the spider webs from my eyes, I strain to look in Charlie's direction. His cobalt-colored shirt ripples in the wind as he sprints toward our secret place.

Then, I lose him.

"Charlie! Wait!" I yell with a shaky voice.

I am too far in the woods to get misplaced; there is no way I can find my way home. Charlie is supposed to watch me; Mom said so before we left.

Beads of sweat drip into my eyes, burning my vision and blurring the forest ahead of me. I frantically scan the pine jungle for my brother, silently praying he hasn't left me behind. With the edge of my sleeve, I dab the corners of my eyes in the hopes that removing the dirt and sweat will bring clarity.

My legs begin to crumble from exhaustion and fear. Breaking for a moment to regain my composure, I listen, hoping to hear his heavy footsteps.

After countless moments yielding not one noise, I begin to panic. Without a sense of direction, I take off again—running through the trees. Bits of sunlight dance across the forest floor, and I notice a clearing in the trees above. Slowing my pace to a walk, Charlie's figure finally appears at the edge of the water— motionless. Fast, deep breaths struggle to replenish the air to my lungs. The leaves crinkle and break under my feet as I creep toward him, shoving bits of hair from my face.

Charlie's hand flies up, cautioning me to stop. The seriousness of his eyes freezes me in my tracks. A sudden burst of sunlight is momentarily blinding. Shielding it with an open palm, I focus on Charlie again.

"Stay right there, Sam! Don't move," he demands.

Charlie's voice is soon quieted by a rustling in the leaves. My legs shake as I lean on a nearby tree, finally able to catch my breath.

Standing in silence, watching my brother work, I admire him. He is two years older than me and immensely braver. Charlie is a God in my eyes. There is absolutely nothing he can't do. He's always been a big kid, but standing next to me, he's enormous. Maybe I'm blinded by amazement, or persuaded by my idolized image of him, but I'm pretty sure he's above average in countless ways.

My parents always praised Charlie's abilities, saying he's capable beyond reason and wise beyond his years. It didn't leave much room for my 'average' successes, but I didn't mind. I was just as in awe of Charlie as everyone else. From the time he hit his first homerun at the age of 7, to shooting a deer on his first time out in the woods. He brought it home, skinned it and broke down the meat with very little assistance, like he had been doing it his entire life. I figured that sticking close to him would aid me in becoming more capable, but nothing has really rubbed off quite yet.

Charlie regains my attention when he reaches down to the ground with one hand. My body urges me to move closer, but my brain tells me to stay still.

He lifts his hand from the ground, and pinched between his fingers is a leathery-looking black snake, bending every way it can to try and bite him.

"Charlie! Be careful!" I yell.

My heart bangs off my ribcage as I hold my breath, so worried he will get bitten. Thoughts of Charlie lying on the ground and me not being able to find my way home to get help leave me feeling hopeless and terrified.

"Charlie, please!" I beg of him, tears streaming down my inflamed cheeks.

I hope once Charlie hears the desperation in my voice he will realize how much he is scaring me. Our eyes connect before he flings the snake across the pond and into the woods. For what feels like hours, I study his face, waiting for it to relax. Charlie watches the reptile slither away before turning back to me and wiping his hands on his jeans.

"Ok, Sam. It's safe now," he says with a wink.

I envy the mountain-man dirt under his fingernails as he pushes his arms out, inviting me toward him.

"C'mon," he encourages, with a wave of his fingers.

"What did ya think, Sam? I was gonna leave you alone in the woods?" he asks, in an almost hurt tone. "It's my job to always watch out for you, and to keep you safe. That's what big brothers are for," he reminds me with another wink while helping me down onto the muddy bank.

Charlie's lips move into a sort of cocky smile, implying that I wouldn't be able to survive without him. Unfortunately, he's right. With zero hesitation, I walk over and wrap my arms around his waist.

"You know I'll never let anything hurt you, sis," Charlie whispers.

I nod and bury my face deep in his chest. A sense of relief sets in, knowing I am with him again; my safe haven—my knight in shining armor—my very best friend.

"Wanna make a fishing pole?" he asks, snapping me back to reality.

Charlie laughs when a huge grin screams across my face. "I'll take that as a yes, I guess?"

I nod excessively with a wide-toothed grin, showing Charlie my missing front tooth. It fell out the night before, but I haven't gotten a chance to tell him yet. I know he will be so impressed.

"Ah, I see you're growing up, Sam," he says, pushing a clenched fist into my shoulder. "Soon you won't need me to protect you anymore."

His statement offends me. I can't imagine that there will ever be a time when I wouldn't want Charlie in my corner. While I digest his statement, he pulls a thin piece of Dad's fishing line out of his pocket and combs the forest floor for a decent-sized stick.

"Get out of Sam-land and find us some bait," he instructs.

Moments later, my freshly painted fingernails are pulling a worm from the dirt and proudly handing it to Charlie. His retrieves it, and smiles—a smile that could stop traffic.

Everyone loves Charlie, and I am no exception.

"Alright, Sam, now we wait," he says, dropping the worm into the water.

Pulling a small knife from his pocket, Charlie begins to peel back the layers of a fallen tree. I watch in awe as he meticulously carves.

"Whatcha doin', Charlie?" I ask quietly as not to disrupt his concentration.

He looks up, smiling at me while he continues to carve away the wood.

"I'm making us a bench, so we have somewhere to sit when we fish," he tells me, then returns his gaze to the tree.

I brush the leaves off of a nearby log, settling in to its rigid exterior. I feel a tug on the pole, but ignore it. I'm lost in a picture of me sitting next to Charlie on "our" bench; the bench he is making for me. He is the best big brother, and I am so lucky.

Chapter 1

The room is blurry. Colorful shapes materialize before me as I try to remember what the foreign objects are. I have been here before, so I know the main logistics of it, but I am still having trouble. I hover in Mom's shadow while she talks to the sales lady, careful not to wander more than arms-length away as I listen intently to their conversation.

"None of these small frames will hold her prescription. She will most likely need a wider, plastic frame," the woman explains with hesitation.

The saleswoman is overweight and old. I don't need to be able to see her face to know she feels sympathy toward me. Even at her senior-citizen status, she is certainly aware that round, plastic frames are at the opposite end of the 'cool' spectrum, and that I will be ridiculed for wearing them — but there are no other options.

I hold onto Mom's purse, following her to the wall filled with hundreds of pairs of frames. For what seems like hours, I try on one ugly pair after another, pushing my face against the mirror and squinting to get a better look. With a wave of frustration building, I notice that each frame is more hideous than the one before it. Feeling defeated in the never-ending Sam vs. the eyeglass war, I grab a pair from a random pile and hand them to Mom. The black plastic leaves an imprint in my mind as I slide my old glasses over the bridge of my nose, and we leave the store.

When we walk past the store windows, I catch a glimpse of myself: Charlie's hand-me-down t-shirt hangs off my bony shoulders. My thrift store hip-hugger jeans are not living up to their name, and the sole of my left high top is starting to flop against my foot with each step.

Hopefully I can find some fashion sense somewhere down the road — everyone is awkward at this age, *right?*

Hurrying to keep up with Mom, who is already unlocking the car door, I listen as she talks on the phone to Dad.

“I’m not sure,” she starts. “Charlie has never been in trouble before. Did the school say why the fight started? Are they pressing charges? Well, I guess we will have to discuss it with him and make sure it’s only a one-time thing. I’ll be home in 30 minutes.”

“What was that about?” I ask.

“Nothing,” Mom responds with a deep exhale. “Ever since Charlie started high school, something changed in him. It’s just like someone flipped a switch and your father and I have no idea why.”

“Have you tried asking him?” I inquire.

“Charlie has never been a great talker—you know that, Sam. We will just give it time, and hope it goes away. You know, kind of like when he insisted on wearing those black trench-coats everywhere he went. It’s a phase—it’ll pass.”

The conversation ends and I stare at the trees rushing by. Thinking about Charlie, I question what’s happening to my brother and why he’s changing right before our eyes.

--

"Sam, let’s go! You're going to miss the bus," Mom calls from the kitchen.

I hear the aggravation in her voice grow with my tendency to run late. It’s the first week of 7th grade and I am, without much success, desperately trying to tame my wild frizzy hair.

"Sam!" Mom yells, this time from the bottom of the stairs.

I jump as her voice hits me; I know I must hurry. I begrudgingly slip on my hideous new glasses, fighting to hold back the tears. Reaching down, I yank my socks up to my knees and pull my blue jeans over them. Tugging open the middle drawer of my wooden dresser, I search for the black t-shirt I bought at a yard sale over the summer. Listening to the weather forecast from my TV, I know it's going to be another hot day, but on top of my uncontrollable hair and awful glasses, I don't need to give the kids at school the added ammunition of my unshaven legs.

"Jeez, Sam, you move like a snail," I hear Mom say from outside of my room. "The bus just drove by, so now I have to drive you to school," she whines.

Quickly, I grab my bag, race down the steps and jump in the car, ignoring her sigh of impatience while she opens the driver's door a few seconds later. As she fumbles for the key, I stare at her supermodel figure sliding perfectly into the seat. Her champagne-colored hair, that is meticulously curled, rests just above her shoulders, catching the morning light in each strand. When the ignition turns over, she looks at me — her crystal-blue eyes turn slightly icy as she sizes up my outfit choice.

Mom takes a lot of time to look good.

"You know, Sam. First impressions mean a lot in this world. You should really think about that when you are getting ready in the morning," she spits at me.

Peeling my eyes off her, I look in the side mirror at myself. Mom doesn't ever directly tell me I'm ugly, but she sure does hint it. I often wonder if she ever went through a stage like this, but I'm too afraid to ask. Although I yearn to be pretty and care about my appearance, I mostly ache to wear shorts in this blistering heat.

Walking the halls to class, I swear I can hear the kids whisper and point at me. I can feel my chest tighten as I hyperventilate all the way to homeroom. Once in the classroom, I take a seat toward the back with my hands on my lap, hoping that no one sits next to me. The other kids hug and chit-chat as I admire from a distance. I've been shy for as long as I can remember. Mom said it was just my personality. Thankfully, Charlie was always an attention hog, and I could just fade in the background with ease. Perhaps, one day I will find some confidence, but today is not that day.

--

On the bus ride home, I sit and think about how it has never been easy for me to remain unemotional when talking to Mom; tears of frustration usually put an end to any conversation. Her response is always the same: rolling her eyes, ignoring me and then following it up with, "*Sam, you are always making a mountain out of a molehill.*"

Mom is a master manipulator. Most of the time, I'm so focused on her feelings and needs that I forget I have my own. Multiple times I've asked to shave my legs, and before I can even explain my reasons why, she cuts me off. She doesn't care if I'm being bullied at school or losing confidence with each day that passes. She just continues to say no, because her mom didn't let her shave until she was 15. Misery really does love company.

After letting weeks pass and being unable to deal with the strands of hair anymore, I decide to ask again. My nerves will not allow me to walk up to her and spout the words from my lips, so I grab a pen and rip a page from my science notebook instead.

Mom

My hand trembles as it writes the words across the paper. Fear begs me to put the pen down.

Mom can I

I pause and contemplate crumbling the paper, but then remind myself of the cause I am fighting for. Without any more thought, the pen — determined to see this mission through — launches toward the paper.

Mom can I shave my legs?

When I read the sentence back to myself, goose bumps begin to form on my arms. I already know the answer will be no and wonder why I am even bothering to ask. Pushing off the floor, I head toward my bedroom door, pausing for a moment to stare down at the plush-pink carpet under my bare feet as I grab it with my toes.

While reaching for the handle, my fingers brush past the splintered wood from where Charlie punched it two weeks ago. *What is going on with him lately?* My right foot steps back, as if my confidence is planning to stay in the bedroom. Determined to stand up for my needs, I take a breath and pull the door open.

Glancing down the steps to the front door, I realize that every room in this house is laced with a bad memory. Even the stairs have fallen victim to Charlie's recent violence. My brother has shoved me down those 18 steps more times than I can count in the past three months. I've tried to figure out his sudden violence, and why it's focused on me, but I've been unsuccessful. I try to stay out of his way, hopefully the phase will end soon and we can go back to how things used to be. I shake my head and swallow the memories, hoping it will help to dissolve the knot in my stomach. Despite my small frame, I feel claustrophobic in the dimly lit hallway. I turn toward Mom's bedroom door with fists clenched, and force my right hand up, prepared to knock. The paper softens as the sweat pools in my hand around it.

The door slams behind me and I lunge forward.

"What are you doing?" Charlie asks, my heart nearly pumping out of my chest.

Hands grab my shoulders and push me out of the way. Charlie jets down the stairs, giggling and mumbling under his breath. I find it remarkable, and slightly terrifying, that he can have entire conversations with himself, anymore. His voice and footsteps fade as he disappears into the kitchen. I shift my attention back to the door and take a deep breath.

Knock. Knock.

There is no fleeing back to the safety of my bedroom. I am locked in.

"Yeah?" I hear from the other side of the door.

I can always tell Mom's mood by the way she answers; her emotions are incredibly transparent. The classic 'yeah' means she is in a good mood. If she answers with a curt 'what' or mumbling and cursing under her breath, come back later. It only took one time of Mom's 'what' for me to realize the force behind it. When she is angry, her rings do the talking for her.

The door suppresses a squeak as I push it open. Mom's room is small. There is hardly any space considering the bed takes up most of it, but she has this amazing window that makes up for the lack of square footage. It is huge and lets in so much light. The ledge under it hosts a dark-brown cushion, where I slept as a little girl on many nights of bad dreams. Besides my bedroom, it is my favorite spot in the house. I walk over and sit down, staring through the open blinds at a squirrel leaping across the power line. Wiping my sweat-soaked palms on my jeans, I muster up the courage to hand her the note.

Staring at Mom's back, I watch her shuffle a few items around in her closet. As she turns toward me, she remains silent, allowing only her eyes to question why I am in her room. I stand up, thrusting my hand out to her, presenting the note.

"What's this?" she asks, her eyes locked in on mine.

My right eyebrow rises at her rhetorical question, while attitude fills my head. *Um, obviously it's a note.*

"What am I supposed to do with this?" she demands, keeping my gaze.

Biting the inside of my cheek to keep from saying what is really on my mind, I unfold the note for her and point to the first line.

I stare as her blue eyes begin to ice over, daring me to take the note back and leave her room. I hold steady and nod my head, encouraging her to read it.

Mom glances at the paper and then looks up at me. "Absolutely not; you're too young. You will shave when you are 15, just like I did. End of discussion," she tells me, her words shooting from her mouth like a slap to the face.

Disappointment rushes through my body like a drug. Lifting my shaking hand, I accept the paper as she hands it back, shaking her head. Swiftly putting an end to the conversation, Mom returns to busying herself in the closet. Apparently, that is my cue to leave. I walk out of the room, my head dropped, staring at the floor. The door squeaks closed behind me, trapping what is left of my courage on the other side.

Once in my room, I pull a pair of scissors out of my drawer. Sitting on the bed I begin cutting at the hairs on my legs, determined to get them as short as possible, while tears begin to cascade down my cheeks. I know it's stupid. I know people have way harder things to deal with than hairy legs. But, to me, it's an enormous calamity. I need to figure out a way to get through to her.

The scissors stop when my door pushes open. Standing there, refusing to make eye contact with me is my mother, holding a pink razor. I wipe the tears from my cheeks and glance up at her, waiting for her next move.

"Fine," she says with a hint of disgust. "Stop being so dramatic, Sam. You are always making mountains out of molehills."

In one swift move, she tosses the razor on the bed and is out the door, leaving me to ponder what just happened. I hate when she says that. Even though she gave me what I wanted, I'm now drowning in a sea of guilt.

Although I want to sit here and contemplate her motives, I'm off like a bullet down the stairs. Grabbing a towel from the closet, I run to the shower, hoping I can get this over with before she changes her mind. Lathering my legs with shave gel and gliding the razor from my ankle to me knee is liberating. I watch my insecurity rush down the drain with the blurry water. I dry my legs and slip into my pajama shorts, obsessively rubbing over the new independence that they embody.

Tomorrow, I am wearing shorts to school.

--

The buzzing from my alarm wakes me. I fling off the blankets and scan my legs to make sure it wasn't a dream. Yanking open the dresser drawer, I pull out a brand-new pair of shorts. Once on, I take notice of the thousands of freckles that dot my legs. A tank top and black-hooded sweatshirt finish the look just in time to catch the bus to school. Scurrying into homeroom, I quickly sit down crossing my legs. I can hear everyone whispering, but I'd be lying if I said I'm not enjoying the attention.

"So ... Sam's got legs!" I hear from a boy in the back of the room.

The class laughs in unison as someone else whistles. My cheeks light on fire and I attempt to cool them with my sweaty palms. I'm sure my classmates had imagined hideous birthmarks, or ugly boils on the legs of the girl who always wore pants. The shock lasts all of homeroom; every time I look up from my books, I catch someone staring.

Now I realize what Mom was lecturing me about all these years. Looking good really does make a difference. I am less than invisible for the first time in my life, and I'm soaking up every moment.

Chapter 2

"Sam, let's go!" Charlie yells from the back door.

The anger in his voice is more apparent than it was a few minutes earlier when he first told me to get my butt in gear. Ignoring him, I avert my eyes from the mirror, and glance out the window. The winter sun is just starting to illuminate the fresh few inches of snow that had fallen the night before.

"What were you thinking sleeping in, banking on school being closed?" I ask myself as I slip on my boots and coat.

"Sam, don't make me come get you!" he yells.

With increased urgency, I flip my hair into a ponytail and slide my glasses over my nose.

Snatching my backpack and shoving my science book inside, I run down the steps – taking them two at a time – to show Charlie I don't want to make us late. He grunts at me as I open the door and jump in the backseat of his truck. Without waiting for me to close the door, he throws the shifter into reverse and slams the pedal to the ground. The grinding of the tires echo off the quiet streets as they work to find traction through the snow.

"You're such a pain—always making me late!" Charlie barks at me as I fasten my seatbelt.

Feeling ashamed, I allow my gaze to fall to my lap where my hands clutch the one book I couldn't fit inside my bag. Luckily, I manage to avoid his eyes in the rear-view mirror. I know that in order to steer clear of his powerful backhand, I should lay low and try not to provoke him.

As we cruise down the main road, an uneasy feeling begins to rise from the pit of my stomach. I glance at the speedometer; 50 miles per hour is way too fast for these icy roads. As if the car is hoping to prove me right, the tires squeal and I feel us swerve within our lane. Now more alert, Charlie fights with the steering wheel to gain control. I watch the muscles in his forearm tense as he slides his hands back and forth on the leather.

"Oh, shit!" he exclaims, his words boiling out and cutting through the mid-January weather.

The black mustache he sports as part of his goatee follows his lips as he clenches them together. Frantically pumping the brake pedal with his foot, the truck ignores his requests and refuses to find traction. I turn my attention to the outside of the car, just in time to see us skid past a stop sign.

"It won't stop. C'mon ... c'mon!" Charlie pleads with the tires.

My book falls to floor when I put my hands on the seat in front of me, bracing myself. Looking around the headrest, I notice the tree out the front window getting closer with each passing second. With a sharp turn of the wheel, the rubber tires finally grip the gravel beneath us.

My muscles give in and my body bullets — full-speed against the door. Immediate pain blasts through my right shoulder as it slams off the plastic interior. The wind is knocked out of me and I try to whine, but can't.

Regaining my composure, I brush wisps of hair out of my face and push my glasses back into position. Glancing out the window, I try to see what we collided with, but my window is snow-covered.

Charlie's eyes stare from the rearview mirror. A few moments pass before he says anything. Then, he lets out a sigh, tightens his ponytail, slams the shifter in reverse, and backs out of the ditch.

"Chill out, Sam," he says. "I had it the whole time."

Charlie's arrogance infuriates me. Taking a deep breath, I stare out the now open window, focusing on the tree we almost hit. I can reach out and touch the drifts of snow that have accumulated up the side of it.

"Yeah," is all I can force through clenched teeth. He is lying to himself and to me; we are lucky the tires found a patch of dry road. Charlie thinking I am that ignorant warms my blood. The anger causes me to open my mouth to protest, but I clamp my jaw shut before the words have a chance to leave my tongue. I'm not this stupid; now is not the time to fight with him.

For the last few minutes of the ride, I zone out. Charlie has pulled into the school parking lot and is now turning off the ignition. Upon moving, I can already feel the agony taking over as I drag myself from the comfort of the backseat and into the icy morning air. Pulling my sleeve down to inspect the source of pain, my eyes land on the red indent on my shoulder. Without acknowledging one another, Charlie and I part ways in the parking lot; my legs start to jog as I cut through the flurries that have begun to fall.

Once I am through the front doors, I dust the fresh snow from my shoulders and glance at the clock.

8:26.

I jump, realizing that I only have four minutes to get to homeroom, which is at the other end of the school. My feet squeak as I break into a sprint, pounding the linoleum floors, and with each stride, unwrapping myself from my winter gear. I round the corner, my feet slipping with each step, while the wall clock laughs at me just as I recover my stride.

8:28.

"Two minutes," I tell myself.

My feet jump multiple steps, as I manage to undo the last few buttons on my coat. Reaching out, my hand between the frame and the closing door, I yank the slab of wood toward me, pulling the knob from my teacher's hand.

"Oh, Miss Mallon, so nice of you to join us this morning," she says, as she pulls the door shut behind her.

Between gasping breaths, I try to sputter an apology for being late, but Mrs. Oliver, with an understanding nod, just motions for me to take a seat. Opening my science book, I focus on steadying my breathing and calming my pulse before I pass out from exhaustion.

By lunch time, I'm so furious at Charlie's actions that I can't wait to rat on him when we get home, knowing he would do the same to me.

--

The ride home is silent. Charlie pulls off into the grocery store parking lot and puts the truck in park. I watch as his hand coasts through the air before bearing down on my left shoulder.

"You're not upset about something … are ya, Sis?" he asks, tightening his grip.

I try to pull away, but his fingers hold steady. Hiding my pain, I shake my head from side to side, unwilling to make eye contact. He knows my silence is enough reassurance that I will keep this secret, but, just for security measures, he releases his grip and waves his fist in the air at me just to make sure.

Charlie and I didn't have a great childhood. Mom was diagnosed manic/depressive when we were young, and the medication made her violent. Whenever she got into her moods, Charlie was her main victim. Unfortunately, it meant that I was Charlie's. I knew exactly why Charlie has become so violent over the years, but Mom still pleads ignorance. I guess there's a part of me that feels bad for her. I don't want her to know it's her fault, because it may make her suicidal, so I continue to play along. Charlie lets her hit him, and I let him hit me. Fair trade.

Now, Charlie uses that fear as a way to control and he has perfected his skill. I'm terrified of making him angry, so I cater to his every desire. Although I had a plan to turn him in, his fist in my face quickly changes my mind.

Putting the truck in drive, he pulls back out on to the main road and cranks up the volume on the radio.

Once in the driveway, he parks next to Mom's car. I bolt from the truck before he can turn off the motor. In that moment, I decide on breaking the circle. I'm not staying silent this time.

"Sam, wait!" he calls after me, a mix of desperation and fear in his voice.

I ignore his plea and bound up the steps with one goal: I want Charlie to feel the same pain I felt this morning. I glance in the kitchen, but she isn't there. The maze of hallways to small rooms were perfect for games of hide and seek while we were growing up, but now the layout of our house is putting me at a major disadvantage.

His feet pound like elephants, bounding up the basement steps behind me, as I yell for Mom. I struggle to breathe as I pause, hoping to catch a sound that can point me in the right direction. Then, a faint bang echoes from the laundry room. As I round the corner, I spot her petite frame. *Jackpot.*

"Mom?" I ask, quietly.

Hoping that asking it as a question to see her mood will help, I lean around the corner to focus on her. She's hanging over the washing machine with a wrench in her hand and a pile of soaking clothes on the floor.

"What, Sam?" she hisses.

I know this is perfect timing. If Mom is already mad about something, then she will definitely lay into him for this morning. For a moment my conscience weighs in.

"Am I just as guilty for pushing her on him?" I whisper.

True to form, I second guess my choice. I feel my lips forming the words "never mind," but before I allow them to leave my mouth, I stop myself. The memory of the morning floats into my head; reminding me of the anger I felt; how he almost killed us; how he doesn't even seem to care. Why should I care what Mom does to him?

"Charlie was driving way too fast on the icy roads this morning and he was about two inches from hitting a tree. Then, he threatened me and told me not to tell you," I express.

Before I can take them back, the words jump from my mouth, landing on the pile of dirty, wet clothes.

Whipping around, wrench still grasped in her hand, she makes her way out of the laundry room. I scurry to the side as I shadow her to the staircase. Her perfume seeps up my nose as the wind whips through her hair. It's a scent that I have grown to despise over the years. If Mom is close enough that I can smell her perfume, I know that a loving embrace isn't what's coming.

"Stay here, Sam," she directs me. "Do you understand? Do not follow me."

"Yes," I respond, fixing my posture.

A slight smirk lifts the corner of my lip before an unsurmountable amount of regret takes over.

"Is she still holding the wrench in her hand?" I mumble. "What did I do? I need to get Charlie out of there."

I immediately picture her beating Charlie with the hooked end of the tool, but a noise breaks me from the bloody mental picture. I glance over at the wrench bouncing onto the floor. A sigh of relief sets in, knowing that her fists are the only weapon she has against him.

I listen to her climb the stairs and then bust through Charlie's door. Their voices are muffled, but the bangs are unmistakable. Silence takes a hold of the house, and all I hear are Mom's footsteps back toward Charlie's door.

Standing in the foyer, I realize how exposed I am. So vulnerable. So accessible. I know that Mom has probably released her anger on Charlie, but where will Charlie's anger go?

Quick, Sam, you need to find somewhere safe.

I run down to the basement and hide behind the radiator. Luckily, I am still skinny enough to fit back there with no one being able to see me, just like when I was little. The calm breaks as I hear two sets of feet shuffle down the steps, continuing to match each other's stubbornness. The garage door opens as they pass by the radiator and follow one another outside.

"I'm done with you thinking you can just do whatever you want, Charlie!" Mom screams, "No car for a week. You and Sam can take the bus!"

For such a small woman, Mom has no fear of Charlie, who is at least twice her size. Listening from the basement, I hear Mom return to her mess in the laundry room and Charlie's monstrous feet march up the steps to his bedroom.

"You can't do this, Mom!" he shrieks from the top of the staircase, "You're such a hypocrite."

Something in his voice sends chills down my back and into my toes. I'm not one to agree with Charlie often, but he's right. How can she punish him for something she's done herself? I am certain that just walking upstairs right now would land me a black eye, so I decide to stay put for a little while longer, making friends with a spider building a web beside me.

They would have to be able to find you in order for them to hurt you, Sam. You're safe for now.

Chapter 3

The bus isn't all that bad. The long ride means less time spent with Charlie, and I've gotten to catch up with some of the neighbor kids I haven't spoken to so far this year. I sit in the front with Becca, a young blonde girl I used to play with as a kid. She lives down by the stop sign, in a tiny house with her parents and six siblings. She's quiet, but sweet.

"So, when you're sixteen, you'll come pick me up, right?" she asks.

"Sure!" I exclaim. "I love that idea."

"So, how's Charlie?" she inquires.

My face turns cold. I haven't spoken to him since the day I snitched, mainly because I know he's pissed. It's obvious the anger is churning inside him. He revels in making me wonder when it is coming; like it's some sort of game.

"He's Charlie," I respond.

The bus stops and I say a quick goodbye to Becca as I exit. Stepping into the chilly January afternoon, I make my way through the foot of snow that has built up in the yard over the past few weeks. As I trudge along, bits of it cascade down my boots and melt into the tops of my socks, burning my skin as they disappear. Hesitantly, I meander up the porch steps, fish the house key out of my bag and shove it in the lock.

Trying to shake the cold from my bones, I stand in the foyer, contemplating whether to push the knob on the thermostat to a number above 65 degrees. I decide against it and toss my bag on Mom's old wooden rocking chair in the living room. Peeling off my boots, I stretch and curl my toes, pushing the blood through my veins, hoping to have some sort of feeling in them again soon.

Although I can't hear him, I'm sure Charlie is here somewhere. It didn't really surprise me that he was able to get out of his punishment by catching rides with friends. The rules *always* bend for Charlie. He has this magical way of manipulating Mom to go easy on him. With a wink and lame joke, Mom laughs on cue and suddenly the rules go out the window.

"Oh Charlie, you're so funny," she always says, giggling.

I'll never understand their relationship, and I stopped trying to years ago. I know that Charlie is my parents' favorite, and it's just something I've accepted.

I head through the living room past the family portrait; the fake smiles fill the room, coaxing anyone that enters to sit and stay awhile. *If only they knew the truth, they would run out the door screaming.*

Tossing a piece of bread in the toaster and grabbing the peanut butter out of the cabinet above the microwave, I let my fingers trace the brown and tan veins along the white Formica countertops until they reach the middle drawer. Humming to myself, I pull it open and grab a butter knife. As I tap the blade of the knife on the counter like a drumstick, I wait for the toaster to ding.

Suddenly, the wooden floor creaks. Growing up, I was almost certain that our house was haunted, but Mom would always shake her head and say old houses make noise—something about bones.

I listen for another noise, but there is only silence. Shaking the nerves from my head, I fiddle with my belt buckle and notice that the black nail polish I had applied the night before is already beginning to chip.

Just as the toast pops, I feel hands push down on my shoulders. *It's Charlie.* My body tenses as his fingers squeeze my skin and pain shoots through my neck.

"So, you think you're so sly, don't you?" he asks. His hot, sour breath crawls down my spine as his fingers tighten their grip.

I stare at the clock, trying to make sense of it as the indigo numbers taunt me.

3:04.

Dad is at work for another few hours and Mom is at her friend's house for the afternoon. It's just us.

I hold back the cries as Charlie digs his fingers deeper into my clavicle, his palms easily wrapping around my bony shoulders. Years ago, Charlie was only slightly bigger than me, but once he turned fifteen, he shot up a good foot and gained an extra 50 pounds of muscle. We aren't kids anymore, and Charlie is now the size of a grown man.

Pain turns to fire as Charlie digs deeper. I can't think of anything but the agony, and the need to escape. Staring down at my nearly dry socks, I wonder how much force my heel will have against his worthless old sneakers. Words try to flow out of my mouth as insignificant apologies ram against my teeth.

"I know that this won't mean…" I mumble.

"Shut up!" Charlie yells. "Just, shut up!"

Refusing to wait for his hands to rip my muscles out through my skin, I lift my left foot from the tile floor and, putting all one hundred pounds of me into it, stomp down on Charlie's toes.

"Ouch!" he cries out with more surprise than hurt. "You little bitch!"

Reaching down to rub his foot, his hands release their grip. Relieved that my arms still function, I quickly turn on my heels and take off running. I know my choice to hurt him was stupid, but I'm screwed either way. At least now I have a chance at escaping.

Darting through the living room, I grab the banister to the steps and jump the first three. Placing my hands on the planks ahead, I climb as fast as I can on all fours. Charlie is at my heels within seconds. His clumsy, ogre-like feet pound against the steps as he fumbles to grab me again. His fingertips slip off my legs as I pull them up to meet the step below my hands. My heart is pounding in my throat as I feel Charlie's fingers wrap around my heel.

The sock slides off as Charlie loses his grip. It throws me off balance and I fall to the step. A quick glance shows Charlie tossing my empty sock over his shoulder and laughing at my fear.

He continues to claw the steps below me, attempting to seize me once again in his grasp. This is our battleground. Almost all the fights we have begin and end on this staircase.

His face now matches the color in his eyes as the strands of black hair fling back and forth in front of them. I realize looking back has caused me to lose momentum, and I struggle to put more distance between us. Moving his hands with determination, he frantically tries to snatch me again.

He succeeds and jolts my body backwards in one abrupt motion. His fingers dig into my left ankle like daggers, each of them pushing harder as the seconds tick by. Tiny knives slice my skin, tearing it away.

I turn to him with tears in my eyes. "Charlie, please let me go," I beg of him. "I'm sorry I told Mom," I add, my voice cracking as the fear outweighs my attempt at sincerity.

I hope that the plea will bring him back to when we were younger; when he cared so deeply about me; when we were best friends.

Charlie laughs at my requests as he pulls harder. I am sure my foot is going to detach from my body at any moment. My shoulder muscles ache as I'm failing to keep distance between us. I cling to the tiny ledge of the wooden step. My fingertips turn white as they struggle to hold on. A moment later, they are slipping off the wood in slow motion. Unable to support myself any longer, my chin falls and bounces off the wooden tread.

The taste is metallic and salty and there's no question that it's blood. Forgetting about the pain for a moment, I remind myself to move—to get away, or else my whole body will be black and blue in the morning. As a last resort, I wildly kick my legs, hoping to connect with some part — any part — of Charlie.

"Arrgh."

It works.

Charlie releases his grasp long enough for me to regain my balance and scramble up the remainder of the steps. Bounding over the threshold to my room, I slam the door and lock it, just as Charlie comes barreling behind me. The wood veneer door rattles with every punch. I'm wishing it was something more solid like maple or oak and wonder how long it will hold this time. The throbbing in my ankle begs me to sit, as I wipe blood from my chin with the back of my hand. The door cracks as Charlie bangs his body against it for the third time.

I need to find somewhere to hide. Quick, Sam, get under the bed.

It's so small under there that I'm positive Charlie can't fit. Finding a good hiding spot is key, and it may hold him off long enough to give Mom and Dad a chance to get home. The suitcase in the closet is my usual spot, but there's no way I could get into it with the seconds I have left.

I hurry to the back corner and lie in darkness, surrounded by stuffed animals that lost their way. I stick out my tongue and taste the blood on my face, as I pray the door will stay strong.

Unable to withstand Charlie's anger anymore, the wood finally gives in to his beating. Hugging my knees to my chest, I sink my face into them as my body trembles. There is nothing I can do now but wait for it. The piercing sound of the wood splintering sends chills down my spine as Charlie breaks it from the hinges and tosses it aside. Hairs on the back of my neck stand on end as I listen to his feet slowly creak across the floor.

I know he is taunting me. This is all a game to him; a way to prove his dominance and make sure I remember who's in charge. His black sneakers appear at the edge of the bed close enough for me to touch. I shiver as I tell myself it won't be long now.

"Stay quiet, Sam," I remind myself, attempting to slow my breathing.

Suddenly, the bed lifts off me and I feel the sun's burn on my back. I lie there, shivering and exposed. It's over.

I only have a second to brace for it; there is nothing left to do. Charlie grabs my ponytail and yanks me out of the fetal position. I follow the pain and stand up, blood dripping off my chin and landing on his t-shirt. His left hand continues to hold my hair as his right hand takes a tight grip around my neck. I shift up onto my toes trying to ease the grasp he has around my throat, until my feet lift off the ground.

Deciding my only defense remaining is my hands, I dig my fingernails into his forearms, hoping to draw blood. His grip seems to tighten the harder I try to pierce his skin. Suddenly, his eyes burn through me.

"Never again," he demands. "You will never tell on me again."

As a last resort, I decide to beg one final time. I open my mouth to speak but I can't hear any words formulating from my lips. Charlie's mouth curls up to the side and he smirks at me. The space behind him turns dark as my eyes shift to close and Charlie's voice becomes faint.

I have lost.

Chapter 4

"Where are my glasses?" I wonder, lifting my throbbing head off the bedroom carpet.

The room is blurry, and the house is silent. I blindly crawl across the carpet, searching for my sight.

Why am I even looking for my glasses? I don't want to see what Charlie did to me.

I brush my fingers along the carpet under my bed—the bed that has been haphazardly left in the middle of the room. After hitting other toys and books, the plastic frames bump against my hand. I immediately notice the broken lens as I slip them on over my sore nose.

Using my desk as I crutch, I slowly stand. Leaning on the bed for support, I hobble over to the mirror. Once in front of it, my breathing steadies and I begin to study the aftermath of Charlie's rage. No matter how many times it happens, I never get used to seeing my face mangled. Hopefully this will be the last time.

I wait for my vision to clear and then focus on the girl in the mirror; I'm having trouble convincing myself that it's me.

First glance goes to the strands of hair, pulled from my ponytail and into my face, as if trying to hide my swollen and bloodshot right eye. Moving my glasses, I inspect the cut on the bridge of my nose and then wipe the dried blood from my upper lip. My mouth feels like someone has shoved about 20 pieces of gauze into it, but then I realize it is my swollen tongue making it hard for me to swallow. As a tear falls down my cheek, I bring my sleeve up to wipe it and catch a glimpse of the handprints on my shoulders. I can count the finger marks that Charlie left. My glance continues downward until I notice the purplish ring that has appeared on my ankle.

Tears well in my eyes as I realize it isn't just a bad dream. I let exhaustion take over and fall backwards, collapsing onto the bed.

"Sam? Are you in there?" Mom calls as she walks through the doorway, inspecting the fractured wood and destroyed room.

She glances over at me and then back to the wood again, shaking her head in disgust. I casually wipe my tears on the inside of my sleeve while I redo my ponytail. She can read the situation clearly, but neither of us will talk about it.

"I got hit with a ball in gym today," I quickly mutter. "The teacher told me to let you know that I would be fine."

"And the bed?" she asks resting her hand under her chin.

"I'm rearranging," I respond, quickly.

Mom nods her head one time, acknowledging my story, and moves on. There is no point in indulging her in the violent details; she always sides with Charlie anyway. I now know I was wrong for telling on my brother, and I got a good dose of karma for being a snitch.

"Go clean yourself up and get ready for supper," she says calmly, looking around to access the damage. "I'll have your father fix this when he has time."

Her footsteps cause the hallway floor to creak as she exits. My one blurred eye reminds me of the broken lens.

"Mom?" I call out, heading through the doorway. "What about my glasses?" I ask, struggling to keep up with her as she floats down the stairs.

She halts halfway and shakes her head, obviously frustrated with me for allowing them to get broken.

"Wear your old ones for now until I can get you to the doctor," she sighs, her hips flailing side to side as she finishes the steps. "Oh, and stop crying, Sam. It's not the end of the world."

I roll my eyes while she flips her hair into a clip and rounds the banister before disappearing into the kitchen. I limp to the bathroom, still struggling to breathe. As the water begins to warm, I splash it on my face and watch the blood circle down the drain.

I know she is right. I'll just remember to keep my mouth shut next time.

During dinner, Charlie and I exchange glances one time, and in that moment, his eyes threaten me. With a swift tightening of his fists, he silently informs me that if I don't keep quiet, I'll never speak again. I nod my head, agreeing to his demand, before shifting my eyes back down to my plate.

Pushing the spaghetti around with my garlic bread, I listen to Mom and Charlie while they chat about the upcoming baseball season. I see my escape and proceed to shovel the remaining food in my mouth. Before I can swallow, I ease my chair backwards on the shaggy burgundy carpet. Mom halts her conversation when she catches my movement in her peripheral vision. Looking in my direction, she clears her throat, making sure I understand that she is annoyed with me leaving the table.

"May I be excused?" I mumble, unwilling to lift my sights from the frayed edges of the carpet.

Mom dismisses me with a wave of her fork.

When I climb the stairs to my bedroom, each step reminds me of the afternoon's events. Once inside, I decide I don't have enough energy to change into my pajamas, so I retreat under the covers fully clothed. I place my glasses on my nightstand before pulling the blankets over my eyes. The painful aches in my body are not enough to keep me awake, and I feel my mind slowly drift off.

I fall asleep to the sound of Mom and Charlie's giggles, floating up the stairs and through the vacant doorway to my room. A final shiver runs through my body as I swallow the idea that they have finally claimed the last safe place left in this house.

Chapter 5

My wrist bends when I lay my head on it in the doctor's chair, waiting for him to return. The room is dimly lit and small, illuminated only by a white screen filled with black letters in no particular order. Next to me, Mom turns the pages in her gossip magazine as I squint to make out the characters on the screen. There's movement in the room, and out of the corner of my eye, I watch my mother's blurry shape stand and roam into the hallway.

"Where is this guy?" she impatiently asks to no one in particular.

Totally embarrassing. Hunching down in the seat I hope to disappear into the darkness.

"Don't these people know I have to get dinner ready and wash Charlie's uniform for his game tomorrow?" she hisses.

Mom's right hand rises into the air as she flags down a nearby nurse. I sit completely motionless, hoping to camouflage into the fabric of the chair while the young innocent woman works to appease my mother.

"The doctor will be right in, ma'am. I apologize for the wait. It's been a very busy day," she responds, obviously intimidated by my platinum-blonde fireball of a mother.

Realistically, it has only been a few minutes since the doctor finished my exam and walked out of the room, but it's far too long for Mom's liking. With each passing moment, the tension in the room becomes heavier. After counting the repetitive clicks of Mom's black knee-high boots to somewhere around 80, the doctor reenters. My eyes cut through the darkness as I search for her and beg to keep her comments to herself.

"It's about time," she mumbles under her breath, just loud enough for him to hear.

I let out a heavy sigh. Out of the long list of qualities I pray aren't genetic, impatience is high on the list.

Ignoring her statement, the doctor takes a seat. His soft eyes come into focus as he rolls closer to me. Fed up with how long this is taking, Mom leaves the room to text Charlie.

"I'm sorry," I mumble toward him, quietly apologizing for Mom's behavior.

After a slight giggle, he smiles and shakes his head, "No worries, my dear. Let's get started, shall we? First, Miss Samantha, I need you to tilt your head back," he tells me as he searches for something on the nearby table. "I'm going to hold your eye open and place the contact in," he continues, holding the circular piece of plastic for me to study. While his shaky hands demonstrate the process, my palms begin to sweat. "It may burn, but I want you to blink a few times. Just resist the urge to rub."

His hand—as cold as ice—touches my chin to position my head. I strain to keep my eye open as his finger jabs it several times. Fire burns as the contact enters. I immediately regret this choice.

"Please, take it out!" I beg. "It hurts too badly. I can't do this."

"Bear with me, Samantha. It will calm down. Give it a second. Take a deep breath," he encourages. "This is normal. There's nothing wrong, just part of the process."

Gripping the armrests of the chair, the tears are building, preparing to cascade like waterfalls down my cheeks. The agony is almost unbearable as I begin to panic.

"Try to blink. It will help with the pain," he reminds.

I force myself to blink a few times, and the pain begins to subside as the saline pushes the lenses overtop my pupil. The doctor's voice rings through my temporary blindness.

"Ok, Miss Samantha, continue to blink until they feel steady," he instructs. I try to remain focused on his directions as he pushes the other contact into my eye.

The fire burns again, but I blink more readily, and it fades much faster than last time. *How the hell am I supposed to do this myself*?

"When you are ready, you can go ahead and look in the mirror," he coaxes. "I think you will be pleased."

Things are still a little blurry. As I begin to question the clarity of contacts in general, the words on Mom's magazine become legible. Gazing my newly acquired vision around the room, my eyes drink in all the things that were blind to me only moments ago. My glance ricochets from the wall of eye drops to the garbage can littered with empty bottles in the far corner. Remembering the mirror in my hand, I lift it in front of me to get a glance of my glassless face.

"Don't worry about the redness in your eyes," the doctor explains. "It'll fade. And your eyes will get used to it over time."

Feeling slightly self-conscious, I catch eyes one last time with the gray-haired man in front of me.

"How do they feel, Miss Samantha? A bit different, I bet." His words flow genuinely as he inches closer to examine them once more.

My teeth explode through my lips as the corners of my mouth reach toward my ears. "They feel great!" I exclaim as my voice cracks, and my body rocks back and forth from excitement. "I love them!"

I catch a glimpse of Mom out of the corner of my eye; a common displeased expression covers her face, but I choose to ignore it.

As the doctor switches on the fluorescent light above me, my glasses stare at me from the light brown countertop. I look away, gather myself, and realize that a new phase has begun. With a pronounced sigh, I release the shame and resentment I've been holding onto for years.

Mom's toe impatiently clicks on the floor, forcing me out of my gawking and back into the reality of the exam room. Remembering she is already on edge, and wanting to avoid any altercation, I place the mirror down on the counter and scurry to follow her out the door.

The engine of the car purrs in the background as Mom starts it up. My legs are barely in the door as the wheels begin to roll backwards and I click my seatbelt, a giant smile still engulfing my face.

Then I feel it. My left cheek burns as it catches the fire from Mom's stare.

"I expected you to look a lot prettier without your glasses than you do," she says, matter-of-factly. Her lips show a tight pucker as I notice the lines of her lipstick are slightly smudged.

Ignoring her hostility, I stare at the girl in the side mirror, proving to myself that it's actually me. As I shift it from side to side inspecting all angles, a sense of pride begins to surface.

"Well, I think I look good," I tell her, regretting the words as soon as they leave my mouth. I yank on my ponytail and auburn locks fall sporadically as my confidence continues to grow.

"Well, I guess we are quite confident in ourselves now, aren't we?" Mom says, begging me to take her bait.

"It seems so, doesn't it?" I respond.

Hook, line and sinker.

The blow of Mom's rings ends my short streak of courage. I lick my lip, noticing the familiar taste of blood.

"Don't be so obnoxious, Sam," she tells me, fixing her rings and returning her hand to the steering wheel. "It's what gets you in trouble."

I flip my hair back up into a messy bun, before smoothing down any bumps with the sweat from my palms. The headrest serves as a home for my head while I stare out the window, hoping it will subdue the rage building on my face.

"I'm sorry," I tell her, a hint of anger hanging off of my half-hearted apology.

She nods her head in approval, a simple gesture that reminds me she is the leader of this pack. I look down at my hands folded in my lap and notice the streak of red smear on my right thumb. I remember the blood on my lip and clean up the cut with a napkin I pull out of the glove box. I sneak one last glance in the mirror to confirm the swelling that has already begun to surface.

--

The frosty breeze blasts my face as I open the freezer and search, deep in the back corner, for my ice pack. My lip burns from the cold before the ice numbs the pain. One of these times I expect to be immune to the sting.

I close the freezer and head toward the living room. Charlie barrels down the stairs as I round the corner. Remaining focused on the uneven tread of the wood floor as I pass him, the blow of his shoulder into mine knocks me off my path. Glaring my eyes into his, I fix my ice pack.

"You think you'd learn one of these times to keep your mouth shut, Sam," he snorts, continuing toward the kitchen.

Maybe he's right.

I shake the thoughts from my mind and place one foot in front of the other up the stairs to my room. My blankets summon me, but before giving in I remember to remove and stow my new contacts.

Once under the covers and certain I'm alone, I shift onto my side and stare off into the blurry darkness. The curtain Mom uses to hide my closet is blowing, and my body won't allow my eyes to trust it's just the wind. The glow under my door from the hallway light clicks off and the curtain becomes lost in the darkness.

Fear engulfs me.

I pull the blankets to cover my head, and listen for any sound of footsteps across my bedroom floor. Knowing that every noise will keep me awake, I sink down into the crevice that has formed between my mattress and the wall, hoping it will keep me safe for another night.

Chapter 6

"All students please report to their homeroom classes. This is your two-minute warning," the principal's voice directs over the loudspeaker.

I slam my locker shut while a nearby teacher mimics the announcement. My eyes burn from struggling to put my contacts in all morning, and I hope the hall-monitor doesn't think I was smoking a joint on the ride in. I brush my side bang from my eyebrow as I slide through the doorway to homeroom.

"Did you have to touch your eyes to put those things in?" Susie, a brown-haired girl in the chair behind me asks, poking her eyelid as she waits for my acknowledgment.

"It's not too bad," I tell her, shrugging my shoulders.

Steady blinking helps hydrate my lenses and ease the burn while Susie turns and whispers something to the girl behind her. A strange feeling rises in my chest with the attention I'm gaining now that I've gotten rid of my glasses. It surprises me how shallow people can be.

"Please, quiet down class," Mrs. Dever says as she pulls the door shut, locking anyone who is late on the other side.

Susie's metal chair squeaks on its front legs as she leans forward. "You look pretty, Sam," she whispers in my ear.

I turn and thank her with a smile. She gathers her hair in her hands and flips it behind her shoulders. Fire ignites in my cheeks. I can't remember anyone ever describing me as "pretty".

I feel a pair of eyes burning through me as a glare from the front of the room catches my attention. Without moving my head, I slowly lift my glance from my notes. Violet eyes scowl at me as Stephanie, the most popular girl in class, tries to break me down with her stare. My eyes fall back to the safety of my notes, but Steph holds strong. *Is she staring at me, or am I just caught in the crossfire?*

A few minutes later, I slowly raise my eyes and connect with hers again —she doesn't flinch. Instead, her eyes travel from the top of my head down to my shoes and back up again, ending where she began. Just before breaking her stare, she slips into a slight smile and flips her too-blonde curls over her shoulder, turning back to face the board.

The anxiety from the moment has caused my palms to sweat, so I wipe them on my jeans. Focusing back to Mrs. Dever, I feverishly scribble in my notebook, struggling to catch up.

Half an hour later, tingles race up and down my arm as it starts to fall asleep from resting my head on it. I love Mrs. D, but sometimes her class is a real snooze fest. Needing a break, I glance at the wooden hall pass sitting on the ledge of the chalkboard and my hand rises. Mrs. D nods her head at me before I can even ask to use the lavatory. Quietly I exit the room, assisting the door shut as I make my way to the restroom.

Glancing into the chipped bathroom mirror, the freezing cold water runs over my hands. Leaning in closer to inspect my eyes, I notice they are no longer as inflamed as they were this morning. Pleased with how normal I am beginning to look, I sneak a smile at the girl staring back at me.

As I turn the corner to exit, I nearly collide with the girl entering. The scent of vanilla-bean perfume engulfs me as I side-step to go around her. A high-heeled black boot blocks my path when she jams it in front of me like a roadblock. She scrutinizes me for the second time today, criticizing every inch with her stare.

"So, what? You think you're competition for me or something since you're not wearing those disgusting glasses?" she asks.

I wrack my brain for a witty comeback, but it comes up blank. Her voice is smooth as it continues to spit insults.

"Even without glasses, your hair is still frizzy, your clothes are gross, and you smell weird," she sneers at me, adding, "I don't even know why you bother."

I nod, like a pathetic child, showing her that I agree with every statement out of her mouth. She is ripping me apart and I don't have the courage to do anything about it. Most of her words are sliding in one ear and out the other while I wait for it to end, until it slaps me in the face.

"Just remember, you never have—and never will—be pretty."

She strikes a nerve with her final words. I know fighting back will give her exactly what she's looking for, so instead, I walk away. Her boot blocks my path and throws me off course. As her hand pushes on the small of my back, I plummet to the ground. Unable to react quick enough to regain my balance, my nose—feeling like it's shattering to pieces—hits the concrete first. Unfortunately, Steph's voice is the first sound breaking through the echo of my collapse.

"Someone, help!" she screams through the empty hallway.

I listen to her boots click on the linoleum as she runs to the nearest classroom and rips open the door. A middle-aged man emerges and immediately notices the emergency.

"Call the nurse!" he screams to a nearby hall monitor.

My head pounds as the voices reverberate off the walls. With little effort, I raise myself to a sitting position. *That little bitch has no idea what I deal with on a regular basis.* As the tears clear, I notice a few drops of blood on the floor beneath me. Brushing the hair from my face causes a whirlwind of vanilla perfume to once again swirl up my nostrils. Groans sneak out under my breath when I notice a well-rehearsed false sense of worry on Steph's face.

The whine of the wheelchair startles me as the nurse pushes it in my direction. She alternates glances between my bleeding nose and Steph's pouting eyes, hoping one of us will give her an honest recollection of events.

"What happened here ladies?" she asks, placing my chin in her fingers and moving it from side to side, accessing the damage.

I open my mouth to speak but I'm too slow.

"I was walking to the bathroom when I saw Sam slip and fall onto the floor," Steph tells the small crowd of teachers and administrators that have circled us. "The janitors should really put signs up if the floor is wet. That's very unsafe. I ran over to help and then went to get the teacher as quickly as I could."

Her lie is not surprising; Steph didn't get to the top of the popularity pool by being a sweet and honest girl. I sit in silence, holding a tissue against my nose as she spews words of concern.

"I hope the fall didn't hurt her too bad. She's so pretty. I wouldn't want anything to ruin that for her."

Anger bubbles through me and I fight the urge to pummel her into the concrete. The throbbing pain of my nose wins over the need to tell the truth. Tears I've been holding back escape my eyes and evaporate as they travel down my inflamed cheeks. It's not a battle I have the energy to fight. Today, Steph wins.

The nurse places her hands under my arms and assists me to the chair. Steph offers us a princess wave upon exiting. I drop my hand to the side, and allow one finger to rise, making sure she knows exactly how I feel about her.

My face will one day grow immune to the sensation of ice touching it, but not today. While I lay in the dark room waiting for Mom to pick me up, I think about the crappy ice pack the school gave me, and how I wish I had mine from the freezer at home. My eyes flicker open when the curtain slides on the metal bar and Mom's face peeks in.

"Oh, Sam … sweetie, are you ok?" she asks. Her sense of worry is almost convincing me that she cares.

Genuine or not, Mom's presence comforts me. I soak up all the fake love and lean in as she bends down to hug me, something I haven't felt in years. I resist as she pushes me away only moments later.

"Time to go, Sam," she instructs as she unwraps my arms from her torso. "That's enough, now."

Her arm is flung over my shoulder, supporting me, while we walk out through the front doors to the car. For a moment, I feel like we are bonding. Yet, as quickly as it began, the connection is ripped from my grasp as she pushes me into the car and slams the door shut. Turning the key in the engine, she pauses to look at me.

"This is what I told you would happen when you got those contacts," she sighs. "You got snotty and got yourself into trouble. It's better to be invisible; you should've just stayed that way."

My nose throbs as I swallow down the lump of guilt in my throat, trying to push back the tears.

"I'm sorry, Mom," I tell her, hoping she catches the sincerity in my voice. "You were right."

I stare out the window while the school drifts away into the background. Judging her profile, she doesn't seem to be as upset with me as I thought which is reassuring. Sitting in the passenger seat, hoping she'll take care of me when we get home—like she used to when I was little—I stare at her. Somewhere in there she loves me, I know it. I just have to remind her of it. Life gets in the way. Teenagers are harder to hold.

Trying to relax, I hum along to the song on the radio as Mom parks the car at the backdoor of our house. After unclipping my seatbelt, I turn to her, hoping the desperation in my face reminds her of that little girl she used to cherish.

"I have to run up to your dad's work for a while," she says, with little emotion. "They are hiring some new people and need my help," she adds, shifting the car into reverse. "I'll be home later."

I struggle to hide the disappointment as I grab my book bag from the backseat and slowly close the car door, hoping my pathetic movements will change her mind. Before I can even get inside, Mom's car is back out on the main road.

I trudge up the steps, tears cascading down my cheeks as I allow the stress from the day to unfold. After washing my hands in the sink, I peel each lens off my eye and put it away. Pulling my glasses out of their gray carry case, I feel defeated as I push them over my nose again. Turning away from the mirror in shame, I catch a glimpse of my hideous reflection. Frustration burns my face and I bury it in my hands. It was a tease getting those contacts, and now I realize that I will forever be labeled as the ugly girl with glasses, always getting in trouble for her mouth.

Chapter 7

Steph's giggles push their way to the back of the classroom. Her power over our classmates never ceases to amaze me.

Attempting to ignore her, I answer Susie's questions about my injury. "I slipped on the wet floor in the bathroom," I explain. "I guess it's broken. My eyes are so sore that I can't get my contacts in."

Susie acts concerned as she focuses on the thick glasses that have once again made home on the bridge of my nose.

"I'm not sure how long it'll be until my eyes will tolerate the lenses again," I whine.

Our conversation falls silent when Mrs. D bangs on the chalkboard with a ruler. She scans the room. When her eyes land on me, she raises her right hand to her chest and covers her heart. I lift my eyebrows, curious as to what she is doing, just before she mouths the words, "I'm sorry," in my direction.

Abruptly, she disconnects our glance just prior to slamming the ruler down on Steph's desk. A sea of blonde curls bounce with cheerleader pep as she jolts up in her seat. My ear drums burst from the sheer pitch of her tiny scream.

Even if Mrs. D is the only other person in this world that knows who Steph really is, one is enough.

"Treason!" Mrs. D barks at the class as she bends over, her eyes now level with Steph's. "I think that would be an appropriate subject for today's lesson, Stephanie, don't you?"

The corners of Mrs. D's eyebrows elevate, and wrinkles line her forehead. She patiently keeps her position, challenging Steph into admittance. I watch in awe, maintaining my silence from the back of the room.

Steph retreats quickly, breaks her stare with Mrs. D, and begins copying the notes from the board. Mrs. D returns to her desk, rolling her chair along across the floor. Seemingly pleased with herself, she plops down and sneaks a wink in my direction.

I smile, not entirely focused on her words, as Mrs. D begins the lesson.

"Since the dawn of time, people have gone against their own kind to get ahead in life," she starts.

My ears perk up, as do most of my classmates'.

"This act, back in the old days, was often punishable by death," she adds.

Sure, the idea crossed my mind, but it was only hypothetical. There is no reason to punish Steph, when we all know that her perfection is bound to eventually self-destruct. Even a beautiful rose only blooms for a short while before withering up.

The lesson breezes by. I spend most of it daydreaming about Steph falling into a pile of mud and everyone laughing. I'm so caught up in my revenge scheme that I don't notice Mrs. D slowly approaching my desk.

"Patience, my dear," she whispers, coasting by my seat, trickling her fingers across the top of my notebook.

It comforts me knowing that in this moment, Mrs. D and I have some sort of unsaid unity. However, my interest begins to dwindle when my nose starts to throb, begging for me to change the bandage.

I don't want to interrupt the lesson, so I quietly stand and walk toward the wooden pass resting on the edge of Mrs. D's desk. She has told me since the altercation that she will allow me to go to the bathroom without asking if the pain becomes intolerable. It isn't the first time she has offered it to me; a similar request was muttered at the beginning of the year after she noticed a bruise on my neck from Charlie that I had failed to cover properly. Every day there is a part of me that struggles with the thought of confiding in Mrs. D, but the fear of her betrayal always holds me back. I grab the hall pass, ignoring Steph's evil glance while I push the wooden door open, and shuffle my feet into the hallway.

The bandage pulls at the injury while I peel it away. Studying the cut in the mirror, I gawk at the fresh pink skin that has begun to form around its edges. A paper towel works to clean the lenses of my glasses, while I let the cut breathe. After applying a new bandage, I exit the bathroom.

Like deja-vu, vanilla musk fills my nostrils. Her blonde curls bounce as I notice her too-short skirt flapping against her thighs with each step she takes toward the front office. Turning on her heels when she hears my shoes tread the floor behind her, our eyes lock. Her perfectly aligned cheek bones are illuminated with the morning sun that is streaming through a nearby window.

"Oh, it’s just you, four eyes,” she snickers. “I thought it might be someone who actually matters."

Her eyes leave my stare as she turns around, and with a big smile, Steph shows off her signature hair flip. As she prances away from me, fever bursts through my body, calling for a rise to action. Without thinking, I take off, full force down the hall as my feet carry me toward her. There is no time left for rationality now— I am running on full-blown emotion.

Unable to control myself, my hands lift to grab her curls, my body lunging forward. My glasses slide down my nose and all I see is a blurry red surrounding Steph’s tiny body.

A look of fear takes the place of her previous smirk when she realizes I am only seconds away from destroying her pretty face. She turns to run, and the tips of her hair slip between my fingers. My other hand grabs her shirt, but she pulls away. I reach again, connecting with her blonde strands, clenching my fist to hold on to them as I prepare to yank back.

Suddenly, my feet lift off the ground. The room circles and I lose Steph's silhouette in my view. Three wispy strands of blonde hair are trapped between my fingers. Disappointed and agitated, I peel at the hands wrapped around my waist and let out a grunt of frustration, completely annoyed at the fact that she is getting away.

"Stop flailing and I'll put ya down!" he orders me.

That's a boy's voice, I realize.

My body becomes rigid, surprised by his touch. After the shock wears off, I recognize how exhausted I am and fall limp in his arms.

My feet connect with the floor as I fix my shirt and wipe the hair out of my face. Turning around and pushing the glasses back up on my nose, I sneak a quick glance at the boy who ruined my attack. When he speaks again, I get chills.

"That girl's gonna have a life full of problems," he says, nodding his head in Steph's direction. "She's already miserable. Don't give her the satisfaction of controlling you, too. My name's Jake," he states confidently, reaching out his hand to insinuate a shake.

Feeling quite embarrassed and a little confused, I offer a sweaty palm. He gives it a quick shake as I allow myself to get a good look at him.

He's quite a bit taller than me, but nowhere near Charlie's height. His light hair and eyes are soft and welcoming, but hardly noticeable behind his huge nose. I watch as he bends over and chivalrously picks up my hall pass. Our fingers brush as he hands it to me.

"I'm Sam," I say, with a squeaky voice.

He stares at my nose and my glasses, and then scans my body up and down as I readjust my pants.

"Oh, I know who you are," he says, coyly.

His lips turn into a side smirk as if he's holding back a smile. I roll my eyes and start to walk away, not in the mood to be verbally attacked by yet another person today.

"I wish you would've just let me destroy her," I mumble to him, refusing to make eye contact while I head to the stairwell.

My heart pounds in unison with each step I take up the stairs. Footsteps quickly bounding behind me break my rhythm, and I freeze in fear. I whirl around to see Jake, his giraffe legs taking the steps two at a time in order to catch up with me.

"Words of advice, Jake, don't ever run up behind me on the steps," I scold him, trying not to sound too offensive.

His eyebrows rise as he nods in questionable approval and slowly passes me. I stare at him standing on the landing and judge his motive for waiting there. My mind begs me to retreat, but curiosity leads me toward him.

I push my glasses higher on my nose, telling myself not to accept the comforting invitation of his eyes. I meet him on the landing and stop, waiting for him to make his next move.

"Let me walk you back to class, Sam," he utters, as he shoves his hands in his pockets.

Pleasantly surprised, those were not the words I was expecting. I manage to give him a meek nod and hold back the smile that is bursting to break free.

Outside the stairwell, I stop and lean my shoulder against the lockers in the hall as I try not to let Jake catch me staring at him. Hay-colored ringlets stick out in different directions while he runs his hand through his hair, thinking about what to say.

"Maybe I'll see ya around sometime?" he asks, staring at the floor.

Why does he seem nervous? I wonder. *Did someone put him up to this?* I release the smile but not the questionable wrinkles still coating my forehead.

"Yeah, maybe," I respond after a long silence.

Jake walks backwards until he is out of sight. Part of me still believes this is a set-up by Steph to toy with me, so I'll be cautious. Upon entering the classroom, Steph is back in her seat with a gaggle of gossiping cheerleaders circled around her, listening intently.

"What a psycho, flipping out and chasing me down the hall," she whispers, just loud enough for me to hear, "she should be locked up like her crazy mom."

Her words cut deep into me, and shame pours out of the open wound. The classroom fades away as I remember a time I've tried so hard to forget.

--

Dad, never a man for words, enters the room and sits on the edge of my bed. His eyes refuse to look at me while he struggles to explain that Mom has to go away for a while.

"Your mother is sick," he says, forcing out the words.

"What's wrong with her?" I ask, so unsure.

"She just …" He can't seem to form a sentence. "She just had a very hard life, Sam. She's had things happen to her that we don't want you to have to know about. Going away will help her work through some of those things in a safe place."

Tears fall down my cheeks. "Can we go with her, daddy?" I ask through painful sobs. "I don't want mommy to leave."

Dad wraps his warm arms around me. Together, on the bed in the middle of the day, we cry.

Weeks pass, and the empty house is almost unbearable. We aren't allowed to visit Mom while she's in the hospital, and I'm starting to wonder if she will ever come home. I find my way through the dark bedroom every night searching for Charlie's bed, begging him to let me crawl in. I weep as Charlie reaches for my hand.

"Stop crying, Sam. I will take care of you. Mom will be back before you know it, and everything will return to normal. This is only for now, not for forever."

Charlie is my saving grace. Thank God I have him.

The four weeks she's gone are absolute torture. The hallways are filled with students whispering and pointing. Charlie has been in detention all week for punching John Wiggins in the face after he called mom a 'whack-job'. Shame fills my days as I spend most of them alone. Everyone at school knows that Mom has gone to the hospital, but no one knows the real reason why, so they just fill in the blanks with even crazier ideas than the truth. I used to try to correct them, but I've given up. People will believe what they want to, there's no use trying to change their minds.

The leaves are brown the day she comes home and are paired with a chilly autumn air. Dad pulls the station wagon around back and helps her out of the car. She looks thin. Aunt Sarah always said that hospital food is horrible stuff, so I imagine she's hardly eaten. I run to the back door and unlock it, impatiently waiting for her to bounce up the steps to greet me. Instead, she floats by, her eyes focused forward as she walks right past my outstretched arms. Rejection fills my bones and I turn to Charlie, burying my head in his chest as he wraps his arms around me.

"She just needs time to settle in, Sam. Don't worry; she will be back to herself in no time. Let's go and make her some supper, it'll help her feel better," he explains as he leads me to the kitchen. I can see the fear in his eyes as he pulls a box of pasta from the cabinet.

Over the next week, Mom sits silently in her room, staring out the bay window and ferociously scribbling in her black notebook. I've only attempted to enter her room once and was quickly turned away.

"Not now, Sam. Can't you see I'm working on something!" she scolded.

So, now I wait downstairs, counting her pill bottles daily as they continue to multiply. The shell of her figure walks the halls to this house, but never interacts. It was almost better when she was in the hospital, at least then I had the foolish idea that one day she would be back, and everything would be 'normal' again. What happened to the mom that held me in her arms every night and read me a book from my shelf? Or the one that took us for ice cream once a week in the summer? Mom used to cook dinner every night at five o'clock, and I hated that I had to leave my friends' houses early so I didn't miss it. Now, I'm wondering if we will ever have a family dinner again. Will Mom only be a ghost of that person I used to know?

Charlie finishes boiling the noodles and I dump the red sauce on top. The three of us sit to eat as Mom munches on crackers upstairs—alone.

The following day, he packs my lunch and writes a little note on my napkin about how he loves me, and not to worry about Mom— she will be much better soon. I'm not sure I believe him, but I'm trying not to lose hope just yet.

One Sunday morning a few weeks later, the bottles are gone, and the counter is void of anything related to her "illness." I shuffle my slippers on the tile floor and turn to Mom sitting at the kitchen table, her closed notebook resting on her lap. Expecting her to look right through me, I head toward the pantry for some cereal when she calls my name.

"Samantha," she whispers. "Come here, my dear." She smiles at me from behind her morning coffee cup—I can't remember the last time she did that.

Studying her scruffy blonde ponytail, I tighten my robe and walk over to her. Her hand reaches to me as she invites me to crawl on her lap. I hesitate, questioning if she will reject me once I try. The coffee cup clinks when she sets it back on the table and wraps both her arms around me, pulling me into her chest. Our tears collide as we cry the morning away. Charlie was right, Mom came back and I'm never letting her leave again.

--

Dad only shared bits and pieces of why Mom went in the hospital and cut me off any time I asked for more information. Charlie says she was suicidal, but none of us know the details as to what created her depression. Her black notebook sits, untouched on her nightstand, and I yearn to read the words inside. I'm pretty sure it holds the answers to every question I've ever had.

The drive home from school is silent. Charlie's eyes almost seem empathetic as he stares at me in the rearview mirror.

"You alright, Sam?" he asks.

Tears form, but I refuse to let them fall. "Like you care," I respond. "Don't act like you give a crap about me all of a sudden. It's not your problem."

"I'm sorry that stupid bitch beat you up, and I'm sorry you don't think I care. If she was a dude, I would rearrange her face. I know we have our differences, Sam, but I always have your back. I'm your brother—it's my job."

Unsure of how to respond, I simply nod my head and slide out of the truck as soon as he shifts it into park.

Entering through the back door, I scuff my shoes on the mat, kicking them off without undoing the laces. Half-heartedly, I head up the stairs trying not to overthink the awkward conversation that just took place. Thankfully, Dad finally fixed my bedroom door and I have a safe place to be alone. Throwing my school bag on the carpet, I drop to my knees and reach under the bed. My arms comb the rug, searching for the velvet wood I have hidden under here somewhere. Crashing into it with my fingers, I wrap them around the box and slide it out into the light.

Typing the numeric code into the chintzy lock, I flip the clasp and lift the lid. I shift the contents around in the box, searching for that one picture. Ultimately losing the battle against my tears, I stare at Mom holding me in my unicorn robe the week she came home from the hospital. I loved her so much back then; the safest place in the world was in her arms. I so badly wish I could've stayed in that moment forever, but instead I tremble with the realization that there is a good chance that I will never curl up in the security of her arms again. Mom has never been the same since she came back, and I don't know that she ever will be.

I return the picture to the box and slide it under the bed, securing it in the darkness. Stretching out my arms, I roll onto my back and stare up at the ceiling fan.

Maybe one day I will go crazy like Mom too—maybe it is my destiny.

Chapter 8

Senior year sneaks up on me like a woman's first gray hair; it's quiet and evil—yet at the same time, incredibly radiant.

Charlie has found a new home at college, living in a dorm far enough away that I only see him on the occasional weekend and holidays. Mom, with a new full-time job, and Dad, who is always tending to the business, are basically absent from my life. Most days—and nights—I have the house to myself.

These past few weeks have proved that Charlie and Mom work better as a team than as individuals. Without him here, Mom is much more lenient on me. I can't remember the last fight we had, or snarky comment she made. In fact, it's been days since we even talked. When Charlie left, he might as well have taken Mom with him—she's gone, anyway.

Downshifting, I pull into the school parking lot. After working all summer at the local grocery store, I saved enough to convince Charlie to sell me his truck. His eyes were focused on a new one anyway, so I'm pretty sure I got the better end of the deal. It gave me more freedom to come and go as I please—the less I'm home, the better.

Grabbing my over-sized purse from the back seat, I push open the door to the truck and touch my toes to the blacktop. The sound of my flip flops clicking on the freshly laid pavement echoes off the brick as I cross the parking lot, flattening out the wrinkles in my skirt as I go.

The morning is beautiful. Beads of dew, still resting on the grass, catch the early sun while it kisses the horizon. My chilly skin cuts through the dense fog that has formed just above the blacktop, and a deep breath proves last night's rain is still lingering on the school grounds.

As if my presence demands a grand entrance, the school's front doors push toward me when the hall monitors unlock them. I'm self-confident as I flip my sunglasses on top of my head and walk down the chaotic hall to homeroom. Relief courses through me, knowing this is going to be my last first day of high school is bittersweet.

Being a senior gives me the leisure of taking easy courses, such as first-period home economics, just to fill my schedule. I know I won't be able to afford college without my parents' help, so for right now, I'm not wasting energy on even applying—the less control they have over me, the better. I'm looking for an easy year where I can focus on my social life. As I take a seat at a desk with four chairs, the rest of the class files in the empty seats.

"Hello class, I'm Mrs. Perch," a stately middle-aged woman announces from the back of the room. "And this, my dears, is home economics."

With glasses sliding off her face, Mrs. P scans the class of mostly females from behind a large black stove.

"I know it's the first day of school and you expect me to give you some boring lecture about rules and safety," she tells us, mentally counting the number of students in the class, "but we are all adults here and I am sure you would rather be cooking."

Upon finishing, she pulls her class roster from her apron, her pen ready to check off names as she calls them. I take a quick inventory of my classmates, noticing there are very few familiar faces.

"Today, I have a very 'sweet treat' for you," she says, chuckling at the thought of her pun, then continuing when the class doesn't respond, "we are going to cook chocolate chip cookies!"

At the word "cookies", most everyone's attention is now focused on the back of the room.

Mrs. P smiles, “Glad to see that got your attention. I’m going to split you into groups of three.”

The thought of group work sends a nervous tingle down my spine. My racing mind pictures getting stuck without a group, or worse, in a group with strangers. I'm too caught up in my panic, that I almost miss when Mrs. P calls my name and assigns me to stove 'C' with two other girls, Jill and Katie.

My anxiety is full boar. Hundreds of thoughts race through my mind. *What if they don’t like me? What if the other two girls laugh at me because I’m weird, or too quiet? Are they already friends? Will I be the third wheel? Why is my skirt so wrinkly still? I should’ve worn pants. Well, maybe not pants. Shorts, I should’ve worn shorts. Who cooks chocolate chip cookies at 8:00 in the morning? Why not make pancakes or bacon instead?*

“Samantha Mallon?” Mrs. P asks again.

“Yes, sorry,” I say while pushing away from my desk and walking toward the stove.

Waiting in front of stove ‘C’, a tiny girl with a maroon t-shirt and a cute pair of jean shorts meanders toward me. Her ponytail, shining like the midnight sky, swings from side to side as she bounces through the room. She smiles, standing awkwardly close to me, and whispers a faint 'hello' in my ear. Although it’s still early, her breath smells like chicken noodle soup, and I begin to question my own sanity. *Does everyone eat weird stuff for breakfast in this place*? The triangle-shaped beauty marks on her left cheek move about as she chomps on a piece of gum. Mrs. P heads in our direction just as we slip our aprons over our heads and begin preparing the ingredients.

"Jill? Sam?" Mrs. P asks.

Her eyes are focused on the paper when her glasses begin to slip down to the tip of her nose.

"Katie is absent today," she tells us, "Do you girls think you can work just the two of you? Or would you like to join another group?"

She raises her eyes to meet ours while pushing her glasses back onto the bridge of her nose. I incoherently mumble something, and then look over at Jill, waiting for her to take the lead.

"No problem, Mrs. P. We can handle it!" Jill says in a chipper voice, followed by a quick wink in my direction. She reminds me of one of those tough, tomboy-types from the movies—quiet but confident. She's one of those chicks that all the teenage boys swoon over. The kind that can change the oil on a car while looking smoking hot in a tiny pair of daisy dukes.

She shows no fear as she strikes up a conversation with me, in between nibbling on bits of chocolate chips, talking about growing up with three older brothers and twin sisters. I wonder how awful it must be to have more than one brother to worry about, and how I would've never made it out alive. She asks me about my family and actually listens when I answer, vaguely. Our conversation flows the rest of the period as we continue to find out more about each other. We sit on our stools, munching on our warm cookies, when Jill makes intriguing eye contact with me.

"Wanna come to my friend Colleen's house after school?" she asks with a mouthful of cookies. "A bunch of us are going there to hang out. She has a pool."

I try not to let my excitement scare Jill as I jump at the opportunity.

"I'll have to check with my mom, but maybe?" I say, desperately hoping it works out.

--

The last bell rings and I scurry through the crowded hallway to my locker. Pulling my cell phone from it, I dial

Mom's number praying she won't answer. After four rings, the voicemail fields the call.

“Hey, Ma. I’m heading to my friend’s house to swim. I’ll be home for supper. Call me if you need,” I blurt out.

"You coming?" Jill's asks, her voice swimming through the emptying parking lot. I glance over to see her leaning against a light-blue sports car and the blur of another girl jumping in the passenger seat.

Normally, I would wait for a call-back from Mom. But I figure I can just leave if she calls and wants me home.

"I'll follow you," I reply, shoving my phone in my purse, trying to camouflage the excitement in my voice.

I jump in the truck and shift the rearview mirror to my smiling face. Flipping down my sunglasses, I push in the clutch and back out of the parking spot, following my new friends down the back roads out of town.

Chapter 9

The long dirt driveway to Colleen's house is lined with white bricks and small green bushes that are articulately trimmed to match one another. The house, a light-gray brick-facade with a white roof, is situated perfectly in the middle of an open field. The lot must be several acres as there are no other homes in sight. Out front, a large garden with ripe vegetables sits beside a koi pond. Ceramic, solar powered frogs line the walkway that leads to the front deck. The house is at least three times the size of mine, and I'm feeling slightly overwhelmed.

Shifting my gaze from the structure, I notice a group of boys from school sitting in the yard, waiting for us. Knowing my eyes are hidden under sunglasses I study them before putting the truck in park. Wishing I had worn those shorts this morning, I once again struggle to flatten the wrinkles in my skirt and throw my hair into a messy bun. Colleen and Jill walk over to the boys before I exit the truck. Nervously, I fidget a few strands of my hair that didn't quite make it into my bun, as I shyly make my way over to the group.

I strain to keep my focus on Colleen's house, rather than the unfamiliar faces that are questioning my arrival. My head keeps tilting up to follow the enormity of the building. *I'm sure there are so many good hiding places in there.* I think the brick will never end as it reaches from side to side and top to bottom. The windows gleam at me as I count them in my head.

"Sam," Jill says, her confident voice pulling me out of my window counting. "Come over here and meet everyone."

I shuffle to the group and stand beside her, staring at my feet and fiddling with my belt, all in attempts to keep my hands from awkwardly hanging at my sides.

"Sam, this is Colleen," she tells me, pointing to the only other female present.

Colleen, who runs her plastic manicure through her brittle, shoulder-length blonde hair, is loud and boisterous, barely staying quiet long enough for Jill to finish her introduction. Each of her extremities is adorned with expensive jewelry that clinks every time she moves. Her laugh, which is more of a cackle, can probably be heard for miles. I study her for a few moments as she touches all the boys when she talks to them, before turning to me, her eyes narrowing in my direction.

"Sam? Isn't that a boy's name?" she asks.

The boys chuckle as I shoot a dirty look in Colleen's direction, telling her off with my eyes. Jill had warned me earlier in the day that Colleen can be a little rude and to just ignore her. I remain locked on her while she scrunches her nose at me.

"Ewww," she mumbles, looking toward the boys, expecting them to back her up. Instead, they are busy trying to punch each other in the nuts.

She isn't pleased with my attitude. Working to keep the peace, a forced smile fills my face to keep her from getting angry; I have years of experience of calming people down in these types of situations.

"It's actually short for Samantha," I tell her, sweetly.

Colleen looks confused, but my name doesn't warrant any further explanation. It definitely isn't her brains that the boys find intriguing. My attention shifts to the guys as they settle down. Jill's voice rattles through Colleen's incessant giggling as she introduces them one by one.

"Sam, this is Matt, John, and ... Jake."

My eyes freeze on his giraffe body and unruly blonde locks -- *Jake.*

I was so focused on Colleen that I hadn't noticed him sitting in the grass beside her. The last time we spoke was when he ripped me away from Steph in the hall years ago. I never did 'see him around' like he promised.

His eyes remain focused on me while a smile broadens his lips. My insides do somersaults, and my hands feel like they're dripping out a gallon of sweat per minute as I fumble with my skirt again. If I had known I was going to see Jake, I would've gone home and changed.

"Hi," I squeak out.

My greeting is brought to life with a quick wave of the hand. As soon as my palm opens in the air, I hear Colleen burst out laughing. I turn my attention to her, embarrassed. The giggling stops when Jill elbows her in the rib, silently warning her to cool it.

The smell of Jake's cologne turns my focus back to him, and I notice his body inching closer. I panic and side-step toward the koi pond, pretending to focus on the orange and white fish below.

"Remember me?" he asks, softly.

I nod my head without lifting my eyes from the water. *How could I forget?*

"Yes," I respond. "Haven't seen you in quite a while, though."

Jake moves in closer, kicking tiny pebbles into the pond. "It wasn't because I didn't want to see you."

I can feel my cheeks turn hot. He's so close to me now that his shoulder brushes against mine. I'm not sure if I should move away or remain motionless.

However, Colleen's voice ruins the situation before I have a chance to decide.

"Ok, losers, let's go swimming," she tells the group, as she leaps up from her chair and darts toward the front door.

I race behind Jake to grab Jill's arm and pull her aside. "I don't have a bathing suit," I quietly whisper in her ear.

"Don't worry, Sam," she says softly, "Colleen has a million; you can borrow one of hers."

Greeted by the massive chandelier hanging in the foyer, we pass the kitchen, overloaded with shiny, stainless-steel appliances. The breakfast bar is adorned with a bowl of glass apples, which I'm sure cost more than my truck. As we meander through the living room, the enormous leather sectional looks miniscule in the square footage. A big screen TV mounted on the wall looms over me as I follow Jill to the bedroom. I've imagined living in a home like this my entire life; Colleen is one lucky girl.

I stare in awe at Colleen's clothes while Jill digs through the drawers and pulls out a bathing suit with the tags still attached.

"Here ya go, Sam," she says, handing it to me then pointing out through the bedroom door, "bathroom's down the hall."

I lock the door and get undressed, ridiculing my body as I stare at it in the full-length mirror. Mom's voice whispers in my head, reminding me of my big thighs and small boobs. I slip the suit on, expecting to be repulsed by the look of it.

Sneaking a peak in the mirror, I am pleasantly surprised with the way the black string bikini is perfectly molding to my body. *Mom would freak out if she knew I was wearing this, especially around boys. But what she doesn't know won't hurt her.* I double knot the strings to guarantee everything remains safely where it belongs and grab a towel from the shelf, wrapping it around me.

"You almost ready, Sam?" Jill asks, knocking on the door.

“Yeah, I think so,” I answer questionably, making sure the towel covers as much as possible. Pulling open the door, I swallow my fear and follow Jill outside.

The sun's rays warm my face as I drop my sunglasses over my eyes. After following Jill through a gate, I sit on a wrought iron bench in the corner while she makes her way to the edge of the pool.

"Nice one, John; 8.5 for sure!" Matt calls to his friend, his voice trailing off once he notices us.

Jill isn't shy in her suit as she dips her feet in the water. Of course, I wouldn't be bashful either if I had a body like hers. She throws her towel on a nearby chair before running to the diving board and jumping in, her black hair floating above her head as she holds her nose and does a perfect canon ball into the water.

“Whoa,” John jokes from the other side of the pool, "looks like you girls got a tough act to follow!” He playfully splashes water in Jill's face as she emerges. “Jill’s preparing for the Olympics, apparently.”

I roll my eyes as the hair rises on the back of my neck. *How am I supposed to follow that?* I decide to let Colleen go next, buying myself some time to figure out a plan. However, while everyone was watching Jill do her canon ball, Colleen has managed to slide herself into the shallow end, completely unnoticed.

"C'mon, Sam," John pleads with me, "what are ya waiting for?" he asks as he dunks Matt under the water.

All eyes are now focused on me. There is the option of turning and running back into the house—for a moment I even contemplate it. Pushing the fear away, I leave it sitting on the bench as I stand up. This is my first chance at having friends, and I don't want to blow it.

With my back to the pool, I unwrap my towel. Checking that everything is still covered, I run and jump in, hoping no one can catch a glance in that short amount of time.

The water is cold, but I will stay under forever if it means not dealing with the opinions I'm going to hear upon emerging. Air escapes my lungs and I bound back up to the surface. To my surprise, everyone is silent. I wipe the water from my eyes and push my hair back as I glance around. Jake's mouth hangs open and Matt forgets how to blink.

Jill punches him on the shoulder and winks in Jake's direction. "See boys... I knew you'd like her."

Chapter 10

The dull buzz of the industrial-sized air conditioner bounces around the conversations in the cafeteria while I chew on the corner of my sandwich. Eating in front of people always makes me self conscious; I don't like them analyzing my every move. Strategically choosing foods that don't leave bad smells or small seeds stuck in my teeth, I obsessively wipe my face after each chipmunk-sized bite I take. The less ammunition I provide to others, the better off I am. Lesson learned after several occasions of Charlie and Mom mocking my messy eating habits.

My thoughts are interrupted as Jill mumbles through her mouth full of spaghetti and bread. "Wanna come over my house later?" she asks, as a piece of spaghetti slips onto her lip.

I watch her take a drink of her apple juice and think about all the mean things Charlie would say if I ate like that. As she shoves the piece of pasta back into her mouth, Jill's eyes beg me to say yes to her offer.

"Ok," I tell her reluctantly, swallowing the last bit of my sandwich. "Are you sure it's ok?"

"Absolutely!" she responds.

My answer seems to be enough to satisfy Jill and her worry changes to excitement. She wipes the red sauce from her face as she shoves the rest of her bread in her mouth. I nod along, listening to her rattle on about how excited her family will be to meet me.

"You can sleep over if you want," she slurs, her cheeks still filled with bread.

I wipe a piece of crumb away that fell out of her mouth and onto my arm while she was talking. She doesn't even notice.

"Mom loves having company," she continues, as bits of food swirl around in her mouth, threatening to fall onto my arm again. "She's constantly asking me to have my friends over rather than going to Colleen's all the time."

Praying she will swallow her food soon, and take smaller bites in the future, I zone out.

"What do you think?" she asks after a few moments of silence.

It makes sense. Colleen is away for the week on a family vacation, so our normal stomping ground is off-limits. There's no way I'm taking Jill home to Mom, so this is really our only option left. Also, this seems like the perfect opportunity to bond with Jill without Colleen butting in every second. It is the first time it will be just me and her, and that is quite appealing. I follow her lead and allow excitement to set in.

"I think it might be fun! But I'll have to run it by my mom. I haven't really slept over anyone's house before. You know, besides family."

"You think she will let you?" she asks, with certain uneasiness in her voice.

Suddenly, I worry Mom will say no, and Jill will be disappointed. I nod my head as I give Jill a confident answer. "I can't see why not, but I'll ask her and let you know," I tell her as I continue to nod.

Fishing my cell phone from the bag, the white screen fills with words as I type.

My friend Jill asked me to have a sleepover tonight at her house. We have a Home Ec project to work on for Monday and I figured it would be easier to just do it there. I'll text you her mom's number later if you wanna call. I'll be home before lunch tomorrow.

I lie. I feel like the truth wouldn't be enough of a reason for her to let me sleepover. Part of me even feels that the made-up project isn't enough to sway her. I click send as nerves shake through my body. My head races with her possible responses, and the probability that the question might result in her getting angry with me, or somehow finding out I lied. Seconds later, my phone vibrates. I slowly lift it to my face and read the two letters on the screen.

Ok.

My teeth break through my lips as they reach from ear to ear. Jill shrieks as she jumps up and down in her seat, her ponytail bouncing behind her. She wraps her arms around my neck and swallows her last mouthful of food.

"Yay!" she shouts, "we are going to have so much fun! I can't wait for you to meet everyone."

Lost in the momentary deafness, I float immediately from excitement to worry.

Everyone.

The word rattles me as soon as I realize that I am going to be sleeping in a house with Jill and her family. *Maybe her brothers are just like Charlie, or maybe they are worse. What have I gotten myself into?*

--

The final bell rings and I race to my locker where Jill is waiting. Grabbing my bag, we walk out the door with our arms hooked together at the elbows. No amount of fear can keep me from soaking up every moment of this night.

The ride to her house is filled with questions. I ask as many things as possible about each of her siblings before we get there to know exactly what I am going to be dealing with. I watch as Jill doesn't hesitate to answer honestly.

"Well, I have two older brothers. They both work and have money but live at home still to help my Mom and Dad pay the bills."

Jill plays on her cell phone as she continues to ramble. "Then I have one younger brother who just turned 15, he's so sweet; we call him sugar pie … he hates it."

I begin picturing in my head what her brothers look like—how big they are—how tight their grip is. I make sure to remain interested in what Jill is saying as she continues on.

"My oldest brother moved out for a little while to pursue some sort of music thing, but after coming up broke and basically living on the street, he moved back home," she says, as she rolls her eyes. "Oh, and he smokes a lot. My mom hates it."

The way Jill glows when she talks about her siblings leaves me surprised. It's similar to how I used to talk about Charlie, before everything changed.

"Then there are my twin sisters; they are seven. We have a family joke that Mom spent most of her life being pregnant." Jill's hands form an imaginary pregnant belly. "They are spoiled brats," she adds as she drops her hands. "We don't really get along cuz they get whatever they want. I think my parents got tired of raising kids by that point and basically just said, 'do whatever'," she laughs.

"My brother says I'm spoiled, too. Must be common to youngest children," I giggle.

Realizing we are pulling into Jill's driveway, my hands slide off the steering wheel, drenched in sweat. I wipe them on my pants, as I feel the pounding of my heart from inside my chest. A wave of fever courses through my body, followed by a tightness behind my ribcage; it's the same feeling I get whenever things at home are about to get ugly.

Jill senses my nerves and wraps her hand around my wrist before jumping out of the car.

"C'mon, Sam. They are gonna love you!" she exclaims, her smile ultimately persuading me to stay.

Jill is so sweet; how can anyone related to her be bad? Plus, Mom and Charlie are never rough with me when other people are around, so I doubt Jill's family would act like that in front of me. I fill my lungs with one last deep breath. *Everything will be fine.*

The truck door squeaks as I struggle to push it open, my flip flop connecting with the gravel driveway as I jump down. The fragrance of fresh autumn leaves fills my nostrils as I scan the yard out front. Jill notices my eyes focusing on the bales of straw lining the stone walkway as we make our way to the front door.

"My mom likes to decorate with the seasons," she says, rolling her eyes.

I smirk as I follow Jill inside. Two young girls sit playing in the corner with dominoes, peering over at me with their matching black hair going in every different direction. I offer them a small wave as I push the door closed behind us.

The smell of dinner is welcoming as I follow Jill through the house. Within seconds, a woman's voice yells to her from the kitchen.

"Jill? Is that you, sweetie?"

I struggle to keep up with Jill as she moves quickly through the small room lined with furniture and down the short hallway. She peeks back at me a few times, making sure I haven't gotten lost. My stomach growls at the smell of pizza sauce as we enter the quaint kitchen.

Wooden shelves filled with cookbooks and magazines stretch across the narrow hall adjacent to the entrance. White, farmhouse-style cabinets with mismatched handles run across the opposite wall almost to the ceiling, as leaves of green ivy crawl across the tops. Kitchen appliances clutter the counter where Jill's mom – a messy bun of dark hair, intertwined with silver strands atop her head – stands as she rolls out dough onto a floured surface.

Jill leans in and kisses her on the cheek as she whispers something in her ear. They both turn to me as if mirror images, their smiles matching one another's. Jill softly wraps her arms around her mom's shoulder, laying her forehead on it, gently.

"Mom, this is my friend, Sam," she tells the shapely woman.

I raise my hand into a small wave and smile as her mom's face lights up the room. She wipes her hands on her apron as she walks toward me, arms outstretched.

"Ohh Sam! I finally get to meet you. I have heard so much about you!" she says cheerfully, as her body inches closer. "Please, call me Deanne."

I have never called an adult by their first name, but I will do as she asks. I give her a confused look as she wraps her arms around me and delicately squeezes. It has been so long since Mom hugged me that I forgot how wonderful it feels. I melt into the embrace, lifting my arms around her, letting my guard down.

Deanne ends our hug with a kiss on the cheek and returns to her pizza dough.

"Will you girls set the table for me?" she asks while scooping red sauce onto the crust. "Dinner will be ready in about 20 minutes."

I take the plates from Jill's hands and walk to the dining room. Nine chairs – only two of which look like they belong to the small wooden table – are crammed into area, as a flickering light dangles above.

Jill and I are sitting on the back porch when Deanne calls, "Supper!" out the screened window.

She smiles and hugs each of her children as they enter the kitchen, taking their seat at the table. Jill pats her hand on the gray folding chair next to her, letting me know that it is safe to sit. I place my hands on my lap unsure of how dinner works here, waiting for someone else to make the first move.

Deanne places two hot pads down in the middle of the table. Jill's oldest brother, Tyler, carries a cookie sheet behind her and sets it down. The scents of melted cheese and tomato sauce drift up my nose as my stomach shakes from anticipation. Everyone is sitting quietly awaiting the unknown.

While Jill passes a pitcher of ice water around the table, a small, bald man walks through the sliding glass door and over to Deanne. He offers her a quick kiss on the cheek coupled with a slight tap on her rear. He chuckles as Deanne pushes his hand away.

"Bill, sweetie, this is Jill's friend, Sam," she says with a wink.

My face burns as all eyes in the room focus on me. I force out a smile as Bill nods his head, acknowledging my presence.

"Let's eat," he says, motioning to the untouched pizza in the middle of the table.

He slices the pie into nine equal pieces and hands them out to each person as they raise their plates. I stare at my piece. *Is this all I get? No wonder Jill is so skinny. There must be another pie in the oven. Or maybe a salad in the fridge?*

The room is silent as everyone devours their dinner. One by one, they parade to the sink and rinse their plates. I follow Jill as Deanne reaches her soapy hand out and grabs my dish.

“Thank you for supper,” I smile.

The twins bolt past us and out the front door while Jill and I make our way up the steps to her room. My mind races as I think about how horrible it must be to never have enough to eat. I feel extreme guilt, realizing everyone would have had a little bigger piece if I wasn't here. My heart aches for Jill while we finish the steps and round the corner to her room. Next time, I'll stop at the store and bring a few bags of chips or a box of cookies for dessert. Hopefully it will help Jill's parents out, at least for the moment.

Pulling the door closed behind me, I watch Jill plop down on her bed and open a magazine. I scan the room and notice that, in addition to Jill's bed, there are a set of bunk beds shoved up against the light purple wall. The rest of the tiny room is scattered with a few dressers. In fact, the only piece of floor not covered by furniture is the section I'm standing on.

"The twins sleep in here, too. Hope that's ok?" she asks.

I nod and look away as soon as she shifts her eyes back down to her magazine. All these things are so new to me— so different from how I live. I never had to share a room with anyone, and I'm having trouble imagining it. The only place I feel safe in my house is my bedroom. *Where is Jill's safe place?*

I quickly turn as the door is pulled open.

"Whatta you nerds up to?" the man asks as he leans against the molding.

Tyler, Jill's oldest brother, looks to be in his mid-twenties, but his fiery red hair peeking out under his hat is styled similar to the boys at school. The small goatee on his chin is what gives away his true age. He gnaws on one of the strings of his 70's-style hooded sweatshirt, which is streaked in paint and grease stains, as he waits for a response from Jill.

"Not hanging out with you!" Jill yells, shaking her head from side to side as she motions Tyler to exit the room with a simple wave of her hand.

I instinctually back out of his path and brace myself against the closet door, expecting it to only be seconds before he comes plowing toward her. Slowly lowering my body to the floor, I suck my knees to my chest hoping to become invisible.

Tyler's voice shoots back across the room.

"Ohhhhhh, so now you're too cool for me cuz your friend's over?"

I stare at Jill, begging her to stop taunting him but she doesn't feel the heat of my eyes. Tyler steps toward her as painful memories of Charlie's attacks fill my head.

I scramble to my feet and jump into Tyler's path. We are so close that I can smell stale cigarettes on his breath. The warmth of his body against mine is unsettling as I await the feeling of his hand around my throat. *What am I thinking sacrificing myself for Jill? Would she have done that for me? No way, I wouldn't have let her. Charlie is my brother, and I'm the one that should have to deal with his wrath.*

Worried that the silence will further instigate the issue, I blurt out the first thing that comes to mind.

"Tyler! Jill didn't tell me how old you are," I say, trying to shake the nerves and sound just flirty enough to get his attention.

His emerald eyes remain focused on Jill as he lets out a breath on my cheek. I cough it back at him, unhappy with the second-hand lung cancer I just received. His agitation is obvious, but it doesn't startle me.

"Twenty-two, why?" he reluctantly mumbles out of the corner of his mouth.

I know there used to be a time when I could talk enough to get Charlie to forget that he wanted to smash my face. I wonder if I still have the ability.

"I thought you might know my brother, Charlie," I say as I fiddle with my zipper, "but you are a few years older than him." My weight shifts over on my right foot. Smacking my hand against my leg hasn't broken his gaze yet and I'm running out of ideas.

Seemingly annoyed at my obnoxious attempts to flirt with him, Tyler turns on his heels and walks out of the room. Shaky legs are struggling to keep me upright, so I fall beside Jill on the bed. Feeling quite accomplished, I wait patiently for her to thank me, but it never comes. She continues to thumb through her magazine as if nothing happened.

As the minutes tick by, I try to be patient, but I can't hold back anymore. She amazes me. Her strength and calmness is inconceivable and I need to learn her secrets. The words stumble out of my mouth before I have time to filter them.

"Jill? How come you weren't afraid when Tyler came into your room?" I ask. "You stayed so calm knowing what was about to happen."

I regret the question as soon as the words leave my mouth. It sounds so infantile; so immature.

Jill raises her right eyebrow, confused by what I've said. Knowing I can't take it back, I clear my throat and place my hands on my knees, hoping she will let me in on her secrets. She doesn't even raise her eyes from page 23 as she casually answers.

"Uh, afraid of what? Him telling Mom on me? Who cares?"

She turns the page as she scans the articles.

I am confused but don't want to miss any future information by questioning this.

She continues on, "Tyler gets bored and always wants to hang out," Jill tells me. "Instead of just asking, he makes fun of me until I give in. Joking around and making fun of each other is our special thing; you'll get used to it."

I am finding it harder to imagine the possibility that Jill lives in a family of eight people, without one ounce of violence. Maybe it's the difference between having a mom like mine, versus a mom like Deanne. This home was built on love and understanding, and mine was built on secrets and lies. I've never been one to wish for another life, but if I did, I'd want Jill's.

--

Pink unicorns from her little sisters' nightlight illuminate the ceiling as I think about how different our lives are. The crickets play their music through the screen in the window while my eyes beg for sleep, but my mind is churning too fast to allow it.

After hours of staring at the fan blades circling the ceiling, the sun shines through the window, bringing the start of another day. I suck the morning air in through my nose and stretch my aching-tired muscles. Rubbing the two hours of sleep from my eyes, I pack my bag and head downstairs for breakfast.

"Good morning, Sam," Deanne says with a wave of the spatula. "Do you like eggs? Laid this morning by our chickens out back. I'm making pancakes, too. I hope you're hungry!"

I take a seat at the table, waiting for Jill to join me.

"I love eggs and pancakes," I respond with a smile. "Are you sure you have enough? I don't want to impose."

Deanne laughs, "Don't be silly, Sam. You are welcome anytime. The door is always open."

Bittersweet emotions follow Deanne as she sets an overflowing plate of pancakes, eggs, toast and bacon in front of me. “You didn’t say anything about bacon,” I yell. “I love bacon!”

Jill emerges from the bathroom, her hair now tied back into a French braid. “Bacon is gross,” she snarls. “Who wants to eat a dead pig? Not me.”

She takes a seat next to me with a smile.

“More for me,” I respond as I steal the bacon from her plate.

--

My heart sinks in my chest as I wave goodbye to Jill, sitting on the driveway with her sisters coloring the pavement with chalk. I don’t want to leave. I don’t want to go home. I coast down the backroads hoping that I can escape to Jill’s again soon.

Pulling into the driveway and parking next to Mom’s red sedan, I hope she’s too busy to realize I’m home. Without a word, I creep up to my room and pull the door closed behind me.

My heart yearns for a family that thrives off love and affection. Exhausted from emotional pain and lack of sleep, I give up for now, and collapse into the soft linens of my bed.

Chapter 11

"You know he has a thing for you, right?" Jill asks as she motions toward Jake through the patio doors.

I forcefully swallow my mouthful of potato chips, processing her words.

"He has a thing for me?" I question, wrinkling my forehead in disbelief. "I thought Colleen liked him. I just figured they were going to eventually get together?"

Jill's revelation confuses me; Jake has barely talked to me since we started hanging out, and it seems like every time I look at him, he is flirting with Colleen. I shake my head, wondering where Jill is getting her information from.

"Yeah, he talks about you constantly!" she shrieks as she waves her hands in the air. "Colleen always tells him not to bother, and that you wouldn't be interested." She pauses for a second and then adds, "but, I thought you should know."

Jill blinks at me, waiting for a response. Although I doubt the validity of this new information, I contemplate whether I should investigate further. Knowing that Colleen likes Jake, I can't help but wonder how mad she will be if I offer up some competition.

"What do you think I should do?" I ask, hoping Jill can provide some sort of guidance on the situation.

After a quick shrug of the shoulders, she bites the pretzel stick in her hand and smiles. "Sam, just get to know him and see where it goes," she says, picking up a bag of chips and dumping them into a basket. "Don't worry about Colleen; she'll get over it. It's not like he belongs to her; neither of them has ever made a move. So, in my opinion, he's fair game."

My shaky hands fumble with the spoon as I scoop the French onion dip out of the container and into a blue plastic bowl.

"Bring out the dip, ok? I got the drinks and chips," Jill yells through the doorway as she makes her way outside.

I watch her walk over to the edge of the pool and sit down, nudging Jake with her shoulder before whispering something in his ear. Before I allow the beauty of his eyes to frighten me, I head out to the patio.

Staring at Jake as he dries his curly blonde hair is intense. The water teases my senses as it soars down his stomach and collides into the waistband of his green bathing suit. His skin is so pale that if he were to stand next to the picket fence, I think he would blend in. Warm shivers run up my body as I watch him pull the towel from side to side across his back, his biceps clenching with each tug. Realizing I've been staring too long, I decide to bite the bullet and walk toward him.

"Hey, Jake, you want a drink?" I ask, my voice trembling.

"Sure, you wanna grab me a soda?" he responds, wrapping the beach towel around his waist.

The blue cotton sits right below his hips. His stomach muscles form that indent all the girls swoon over, and I'm no exception. *Damn hormones.*

Grabbing a soda from the cooler, I attempt to cool off. As I pass it to him, his fingers graze the back of my hand. His fiery touch melts my palm into the cold metal. I feel the tingles rising again. Realizing the touch is a bit too much, I snatch my arm back, startling us both.

"Thanks, Sam," he says, popping the tab open.

I peek over the brim of my sunglasses and smile at him as he presses the spout to his lips. A blonde curl falls into his eyes, and it takes all of my self-control not to brush it away. *Get a hold of yourself, Sam. He's not a piece of meat.*

Jake breaks our now silent glance first as he combs his hand through his hair before running over to the trampoline and climbing onto it. Standing above me, he reaches his arm out nods his head, quietly inviting me up. I return his reach and he effortlessly pulls me beside him.

Jill shuffles everyone inside as Jake and I mumble small talk back and forth, both unsure of what to say. I nervously fidget with a stick that fell in front of me, breaking it into tiny pieces, using it as an excuse not to look at him. I know it will only take a moment to get completely lost in his dangerously beautiful eyes.

Does he realize he doesn't have a shirt on? He's sitting within arm's length of me and is partially naked. I've never been so close to a guy before, especially one who didn't think wearing a shirt was important. Is this even appropriate?

I watch a bead of water fall from his chin, landing on his chest. It trickles down, bouncing along the lines of his abs. Circling his belly button, tiny hairs throw it off course. Breaking into two droplets, it rejoins below and follows the path until it hits the towel.

Oh my gosh, I was just staring at his junk. My cheeks catch fire once we make eye contact. *He's going to think I'm a total pervert. What is wrong with you, Sam?*

Jake leans back, resting on his hands. Smiling, he tilts his head back and shakes the rest of the water droplets behind him. Before I get caught again, I shift focus back to the tiny piece of stick left in my hand.

"Sam?" Jake asks.

"Yeah?" I manage to push out, still refusing to look at him.

"Will you go steady with me?" he wonders. His eyebrows rise as the question filters out of his lips, fear filling his sky blues.

"Go steady with you?" I manage to cough out the question. "Who says that?"

He turns from me, clearly embarrassed by the conversation, and I immediately realize that I'm an idiot. I went from drooling over him to tactlessly rejecting him in about two minutes. And, it wasn't even a normal rejection. I was a complete bitch. Pinching my lips together and forcing them to be silent, I take a minute to think about how to rectify this situation.

Sliding my body closer to him, I reach out and place my hand on top of his wrist. He looks down at my attempt of affection as he wrinkles his forehead, questioning my motive.

"Sure," I answer, softly. "I would love to 'go steady' with you," I giggle.

"Ok, cool," Jake utters, through one of his million-dollar smiles. "I guess I should've said 'go out with me', instead. I'll make a mental note."

"Hey, it got the job done," I laugh. "All that matters is the finish line, not what happened in the race getting there."

I match his mood with a grin, breathing him in as he slides his arm around my shoulder. When his bare chest rubs against my shoulder, I freeze. Trying to hide my shudder as heat travels through my skin, I cross my arms.

The pleasure of the moment quickly crumbles away as the nerves seek me out again. I have never held a boy's hand or kissed a boy. Frankly, boys have never even really talked to me. The abuse in my home wasn't just physical. It was emotional, as well. The number of times I heard how ugly I was from my mother and brother, is infinite. Now, I know how to shrug it off, but the years of abuse run deep.

Remarkably, I've managed to catch the boy of my dreams, and I have no clue how to handle it. I start to worry that Jake is out of my league and this 'relationship' will be over quicker than it begins. I let my walls build up to protect my emotions as I keep one ear open to his beautiful voice.

"Just so you know, Sam, I've never had a girlfriend before," he confesses to me. His words remedy my anxiety and help me find the courage to come clean about my inexperience as well.

"Me either," I reply with a smile, then catch myself, "boyfriend, I mean ... I never had a boyfriend."

I immediately smack my palm to my forehead as my freckles now became hidden behind a sea of red, waiting for Jake to take back everything he just said. Instead, he just chuckles as he lies back on the trampoline and looks at the sky, which is now overcome with stars speckling the darkness.

He lays out his arm out in my direction, stretching his fingers one at a time. I wipe the cold sweat from my palms onto my shorts as I lay down next to him. His body swallows mine as I fearfully allow him to take control. Struggling for a calm breath, I take in the moment.

"You know you're like the prettiest girl I've ever seen?" Jake whispers into my ear.

Although I should be complimented by his words, I can't help but think about all the girls at school who are a million times better looking than me.

"Thanks?" I utter, unsure of what to say.

If he is telling the truth, I don't want to insult him, so I squeeze his hand to let him know that I appreciate what he just said.

Colleen's voice shoots through the dark as the sliding door flies open. "Uh, not to break up the love fest out there, but you guys realize curfew is in 10 minutes!" she yells through the blackness.

I shoot up so fast the trampoline bounces as I leap off of it. Colleen's house is more than 10 minutes from home, and if I stroll in a second past curfew Mom will ground me until I graduate. I call out goodbyes as I run to my truck, hoping Mom is already asleep. As I push my keys into the ignition, Jake slams his hands against the car door. Standing outside my window, he begs me to roll it down.

"I'm sorry, Jake, but I gotta go," I yell through the glass. "If I'm a minute late, my parents will flip."

Realizing he can't hear me, I start to roll the window down, his forearms assisting it the rest of the way.

"I gotta go; I'm sorry," I say, rushing through the words.

Jake nods and takes my chin in his hands. He leans into the car, his bare chest pushing against my left arm. Warm chills smother my body as he thrusts his lips onto mine through the darkness. I savor every ounce of his kiss, which ends too soon. His soft lips pull away and Jake stares into my eyes. I gaze into his sky blues as I allow a smile to journey across my face. Trying to think straight and remembering how to drive, I push the clutch to the floor and allow the truck to roll back.

"I'll see you tomorrow," Jake says, as his body slides back out of the car.

As I coast the car down the driveway, my headlights illuminate his body, making him seem as surreal as the evening's events. Butterflies dance around in my stomach as I realize he is mine.

--

The green numbers on the dashboard clarify the time, each minute taunting me as I speed toward home. I shut off the car as I pull in the driveway and coast through the darkness to the back door.

11:07.

Creeping up the basement stairs, I am met with the illumination of Mom's figure by the kitchen light. She tightens her robe around her stomach, grilling me with her stare.

"Where have you been?"

I had 15 minutes to determine the perfect lie to get me out of trouble, yet in this moment, I am having trouble remembering it. The worry that has taken home on Mom's face instills guilt in me almost immediately. Dropping my head to the floor, I allow myself to regret my actions.

"I'm sorry, Mom; it will not happen again," I groan, as my eyes keep contact with the floor.

She rubs her eyes, too tired to fight with me. As she turns and walks up the steps, she calls to me.

"It's very selfish of you to be out past curfew and make your father and me sit here worrying," she mumbles. "I don't know why you would do that to us. I didn't raise you to act like that," she adds, searching for sympathy.

I roll my eyes as Mom closes her bedroom door. I seem to float up the steps and into my room, weightless. Landing on my bed, I flip my phone open and read the texts that have begun to fill the screen:

Jill:

can't believe ur going out w/ Jake! u guys are so cute! I'm so excited for u"

Colleen:

Uh, heard u & Jake were goin out or whatever. lol. that's cool...

Jake:

Hey beautiful, hope you got home safe. Can't wait to see you tomorrow :)

I let out a contempt sigh, filled with frustration as I listen to my parents' hushed voices argue about my punishment, and then about the fact that Dad fell asleep when he was supposed to be waiting for me to get home. They've had the same fight for the past 18 years, always blaming each other for the problems in their relationships. Usually, the fights end with Mom turning her aggression on me or Charlie, but it doesn't seem to be headed that way tonight.

I change into my pajamas and quietly push my door closed as Mom races down the stairs, still yelling at Dad under her breath.

"You never back me up!" she screams. "I feel like a single parent! Take some damn interest in your kids' lives, which includes being the bad guy once in a while!"

Dad follows her down the steps and their voices fade until I can no longer hear them.

I turn my thoughts to Jake, reading his text over and over.

Beautiful.

The word lingers in my mind as I type back, trying to match his heartfelt words. Nothing I write feels good enough, but I continue to respond to every perfect message he sends.

After an hour, I fall asleep to the vibrations of my phone. As I give in to fatigue, the sheet on my closet door ripples in the wind from my air conditioner. I ignore it. Nothing scares me tonight.

Chapter 12

After dating Jake for almost a month, I've mastered keeping my palms dry when he holds my hand and stopped flinching when his arms wrap around me. For the first time in a long time, I feel safe, as long as I am with him.

"Wanna ride with me to John's house?" Jill asks, as she pulls the keys out of her purse. "This is lame."

Jill's overwhelming boredom seems to correlate with the fact that it's just us girls today. Colleen rolls her eyes, shakes her head, and walks inside.

Jill scrunches her nose and shrugs her shoulders, then turns to me. "How about you Sam? Jake lives right up the road. I'm sure he would appreciate a surprise visit from his woman." she begs, as wrinkles form across her forehead.

I glance through the window into the kitchen where Colleen is standing, already texting a backup-friend to hang out with. *This is one of those moments where I wonder if we would like Colleen as much if she wasn't rich.* Changing my focus, I turn my attention back to Jill who is patiently awaiting my answer.

"Sure, let's go!" I exclaim, as I launch out of Colleen's patio chair and sprint toward Jill's car.

As we pull into John's driveway, I study his mom's trailer. It's apparent the beige, fractured shutters used to be white. A broken window – the product of some handyman's attempt to fix with duct tape and plastic wrap – greets us. The front yard is littered with tires and old cars that I'm sure haven't run in decades. Amidst the clutter, John meanders out through the front door, throwing his hood up to cover his unkempt hair. He nods his head before pointing his finger up the road, directing me to be on my way. I exit the car and begin walking, following the yellow lines, as the 'couple' heads inside.

"Don't rush, Sam. We are gonna be busy for a little bit," John calls out to me. His cockiness is so unappealing, and I don't understand what Jill sees in him. I turn back to say goodbye to Jill as John slaps her butt. My focus immediately returns to the blacktop as I head up the road.

The mailbox at the top of the hill is marked with Jake's last name. His house is barely noticeable tucked down in the woods, through a canopy of tree branches. The deck outside hosts a decent-sized hot tub, that still appears to be in working order, and I catch myself wondering why we have never hung out here for a night. Any doubt I have about this being the wrong house is eliminated as soon as my eyes catch sight of the ridiculous black convertible sitting in the driveway: Jake's pride and joy. I knock on the door, praying he answers while I glance around the deck. Brown plants sit in their pots gawking at me, and a string of broken Christmas lights shabbily hang from the gutters. My sneakers crinkle the leaves that have gathered against the wood-colored siding.

"Hang on," a voice yells from behind the front door. A sigh of relief sneaks out when I realize it's Jake. Excitement bubbles inside me as I wonder how he will react.

The door swings open.

Jake is speechless as his eyes coast up my body and freeze on my face. A smile spreads from cheek to cheek. Before I can say a word, his arms wrap around my rigid body and he motions me to come in. I follow him from the doorway down to the basement.

"No one's home," Jake whispers, winking at me as he leads me to his room. I plop down on the bottom bunk lined with pillows and cross my legs. "That's my bed, ya know," he smirks, then takes a seat on his computer chair, mesmerized by the fact that I am not only in his room, but on his bed. The phone rings as I lie back on his pillow and flatten my green sweater across my stomach.

"Hang on, Sam; I gotta get this," he grunts, as he hurries into the hallway. Waiting for him to return, I catch a glimpse of something carved into the wooden plank above me. With a finger, I trace the words as I read them in my head.

Jake Loves Sam

Fear and adrenaline engulf me, and I bullet off the bed. I grew up in a home where the "L" word was never muttered and now here I am reading it connected to my name. I draw in a few deep breaths of air, hoping to calm my anxiety, as I rock back and forth on my toes. Jake's voice is muffled in the background as my heart beats in my ears. I don't know what to do, but I know I can't stay here. Jake reenters the room, just as I manage to push the crazy down and hold it there a little while longer.

"You okay, Sam? You look a little weird," he asks as his eyebrows ascend with worry.

I raise my hand to my forehead pretending to suddenly feel feverish.

"I don't feel well, Jake. I'm sorry but I think I better get going," I explain, holding my stomach. It wasn't a total lie. After reading those words, I do feel nauseous and uneasy.

Disappointed, he insists on walking me back to John's house. The half-mile journey is silent. A few times he attempts to hold my hand, but I pull away. I know my behavior is childish, but I'm mentally incapable of receiving the emotions he's throwing at me.

"I'm sorry," I repeat, over and over. I know I owe him an explanation. He doesn't deserve to be treated this way by the girl he's in love with, but I'm not sure how else to act. I need time to digest this. I need to get out of here before I say something I will regret.

Once secure in Jill's car, Jake leans in for a hug and a kiss on the cheek.

“Text me later if you want," he whispers, regretfully pulling his hand away from mine. "I hope you feel better soon," he adds as he closes the door.

I feel awful as I watch Jake wave to me from the driveway and then shove his hands in his coat pockets, as if trying to camouflage his feelings. John invites him in and Jake agrees, pulling a cigarette from his ear and lighting it before stepping inside.

Silence fills the car ride home as Jill combs the knots out of the back of her hair. I fight with the idea of telling her what I saw, but she pulls into my driveway before I can come to a decision.

Chapter 13

The next morning Jill picks me up on her way to school. Without even greeting her, I blurt out, “Jake carved that he loved me on his bed. Carved it. Meaning it will be there forever. What do I do? I don’t know what to do.”

My words are so quick and unexpected that it takes her a minute to process what I said. I stare at the side of her face awaiting some sort of friendly wisdom; her dimples suck in as she contemplates an answer.

"Wait, like L-O-V-E or like L-U-V?" she asks, putting emphasis on each letter as she spells out the words. "Two totally different things, ya know."

I never even thought of that. Maybe she’s right; maybe I just read it wrong. Would it really matter if I did? I mean, the words are carved into wood. I don’t think you do that if you just like someone a little. Jake is in for the long haul, and I’m not sure if I’m ready for that kind of commitment.

In the fifteen-minute ride to school Jill manages to talk me into figuring out how I feel about it all before overreacting.

“Getting Jake to say he loves you is pretty impressive,” Jill starts. “Even though he didn’t exactly know you saw it, and he didn’t say it to your face, at least you know how he feels.”

I stare out the window.

"I can't even get John to be my boyfriend," she mumbles as she rolls her eyes, "and you have a guy, that you’re not even sleeping with, professing his love to you! I’m jealous."

Jill is shockingly aware this morning and filled with words of wisdom. She is right. I am not even having sex with him, and he still loves me? The idea of it is a little off-center. Is he expecting something by saying it? Did he hope I would see it written under the bed and then sleep with him because of it? I add it up in my head: I am almost eighteen, everyone else is having sex, and we have been dating for over a month. I can't believe that I haven't even thought about it. I was so trapped in my own little bubble, that I somehow have completely overlooked losing my virginity.

Needing time to mull this over, I dodge Jake all day. Colleen pulls me aside after Algebra and leans in, holding her notebook in front of her face.

"Jake asked me to see how you were; he seemed upset," she whispers in my ear, "you guys like fighting or something?" A hopeful smile skirts across her face before she realizes it and quickly changes her expression.

There is a split second where I think Colleen is being a concerned friend, but then sanity seeps back in. It bothers me immensely that she knows Jake and I are going through something, and it really frustrates me that Jake asked her to talk to me instead of asking Jill. I decide to eliminate any thought of trouble in paradise from her mind.

"No, we are doing really well," I reassure her as I force out a smile. "I'm hanging out with him after school. Probably going to his place, if you know what I mean," I say with a wink.

Colleen scrunches her nose, turns, and then heads down the hall, shooting me a quick wave behind her head. "Whatevs. See you later, loser."

Luckily for me, Jake has managed to land himself in detention after skipping class to smoke a cigarette. I can't help but find the rebel in him undoubtedly appealing and am sure that one of these times I will pull a cigarette from his mouth and ask for a drag. I wait after school and walk by the room he's in, casually staring at him until he notices me.

The butterflies swirl in my stomach when he finally sees me and shoots me a smile that stops me dead in my tracks. He nods his head just enough to acknowledge me without drawing attention from the teacher. I smile back, push my fingers against my lips, and blow a small kiss to him. I want him to feel reassured that we are okay, even if we aren't. Besides, detention buys me a few extra hours to calm my urge to flee.

After two hours of impatiently waiting, Jake meets up with us at Colleen's house. My legs tremble with excitement as his car coasts down the driveway. His tennis shoes hit the ground as he combs his blonde hair back and slides an orange hat over it. Tingles soar through my body as he walks toward me and outstretches his right arm. In between his thumb and index finger is a folded piece of notebook paper.

"What's this?" I question.

After kissing me on the cheek and motioning me to open it, he smiles and walks away.

"John and I got to run to get a part for his car," he yells as his feet make their way through the gravel. "We'll be back in like 20 minutes."

I stare at the paper, contemplating what it might be. I unfold it slowly, fearing the worst. *Is he breaking up with me through a letter?* My eyes scroll through his words as I try to make sense of the repeating numbers and sloppy handwriting. It's a poem.

I never knew what I was missing
until I met you
The days were so long
and the smiles were so few
Your beauty engulfs me
as I sit and stare
You sing when you talk
as I float on air

I felt so lucky
the day you said yes
How you picked me out
above all the rest
Sam please believe me
that this is true
There's nothing in the world
that holds a candle to you.
So believe in my words
that are far and few
Cuz from this day on
I'll always love you.

My hands tremble. I read it repeatedly, searching for something negative with no prevail. It is undoubtedly beautiful.

I comb the rest of the page, trying to find the purpose of the numbers. He's repeated the time **2:42,** all around the poem until there was no white left. I wrack my brain until it hits me: it's the time I stood in the hall and waved to him while he was in detention.

Butterflies take flight in my stomach as I lift my eyes from the page and catch a glimpse of Jake jumping into John's truck. My eyes meld with his as I whisper the words, *I love you,* through the air.

He pulls himself off the cloth seat and stands in the doorway of the truck as he yells over the engine.

"I love you too, Sam."

The statement swirls softly through the air before seeping into my ears and coursing through every inch of my body. I fall back into the patio chair and fold the poem before hiding it securely in my pocket.

John's truck coasts out of the driveway as the early summer air blows the scent of freshly cut grass through the breeze. Colleen stares at me from across the concrete porch, trying to bully me into sharing the letter, but it's not going to happen.

I sit for a minute, my hands folded in my lap as I take in today's unexpected twist. Before taking a sip from my soda can, I reach over and grab Jake's half-lit cigarette he left sitting on the table. Placing the filter to my mouth, I roll it across my bottom lip and run my tongue across the moist paper. Holding it between my index finger and thumb, I press it firmly down into the ashtray. As the orange embers turn to ash, I burn away the fear of being loved and loving in return.

Chapter 14

I adjust my white cap as I sit, waiting for my name to be called. A flock of geese fly overhead while the principal continues to incorrectly annunciate my classmates' names over the microphone. I grab a hunk of flesh and pinch the skin on my arm until I wince in pain, making sure this is real; I am finally graduating.

"Jessica Lynn Smith," the principal calls.

This is my row. I stand up, instantly regretting my wardrobe choice of heels rather than flip flops as I sink into the ground. Following the girl in front of me, I try to remember her name to no avail. Doesn't matter now, I doubt I'll ever see her again, anyway.

"Samantha Ardine Mallon," his voice booms through the speakers again.

I trip a little as I step up onto the stage. The assistant principal giggles at me under her breath as I fight back the tears of embarrassment that are filling my eyes. Reaching out for a handshake, I grab my diploma and we both pause for the photographer. Quickly, I exit the stage and return to my seat, my phone buzzing in my pocket. I pull it out from under my robe.

Congrats baby :)

I glance around looking for Jake, and after scanning the stands and almost giving up the search, I find him. His sultry eyes focus on me as he leans his body against the goalpost at the opposite end of the field. Goosebumps raise the hair on my body as I struggle to hide my fiery red cheeks behind my diploma.

Daydreaming about Jake, and catching a glimpse whenever I can, I wait for the procession to end. After all the names are called, family and friends are invited on the field to join us. I turn around to Jake, who has somehow made it 50 yards in a split second. He wraps his arms around my waist and lifts me into the air. Slowly, I slide down the front of his body until my tiptoes are touching the ground and my lips brush against his. My heart bounces off my ribcage as Jake stares into my soul and pushes his forehead against my temple. My body goes limp as I melt into the blue fire burning in his stare.

"C'mon Sam, let's go," Jake pulls me back to reality as he grabs my hand behind him and pushes us through the crowd. "Matt said your brother is throwing a party tonight and they are all gonna meet us there later."

Questioning how Jake found out about Charlie's party before I did, I slide into the passenger seat of his car. There is no time to dwell on the events to come as Jake hands me a bag with a change of clothes.

Wasting no time, I pull my jeans over my legs and yank my dress over my head. I try to hide from Jake's glances as I tease him from the passenger seat in just my bra. His face turns ten different shades of red as I pull my t-shirt down over my chest and playfully smack him on his arm, reprimanding him for looking.

“Shame on you,” I scold. “I am a lady.”

“A fine-looking lady, at that,” he winks. “Sorry that I like what I see.”

--

Charlie's friends are sitting at the picnic table surrounded by smoke as we pull in the driveway.

"Hey Charlie, some guy and a hot chick just pulled in!" someone shouts through the smoky air.

Mom and Dad left right after graduation to go away for the weekend, so Charlie seized the opportunity for a party. An enormous figure steps out of the darkness and flips a beer bottle up against his mouth. His chin shoots towards the handful of guys at the table as he towers above them.

"That's my sister," Charlie says, his eyes daring any guy to even look in my direction. "She's off limits. Don't even think about it."

My eyes stay locked on him as I step out of the car and shut the door. I watch Charlie place two fingers on his neck and draw a horizontal line from ear to ear. I find myself praying these brain-dead baseball jocks can figure out what the motion means.

Charlie's eyes are terrifyingly serious; I'm thankful it's not me at the end of his threats. Although my emotions may be premature, I feel a sigh of relief slip out, knowing he will protect me if one of these guys gets out of hand. I squeeze Jake's fingers as Charlie's focus shifts to him. Nerves fly up my body, but quickly settle as Charlie nods his head at Jake, letting him know that he approves of him being there to watch over me. He ends our silent engagement and walks back into the darkness as we head in through the garage and up the stairs.

"Your brother got a problem with me?" Jake questions while following me through the group of teenagers playing beer pong.

His voice sounds troubled. Besides the fact that he is my older brother and that we don't really get along, I never shared anything about Charlie with Jake. I know he wants more information, but I'm not ready to talk just yet.

"Charlie is just very protective of me," I say, shrugging it off. "I wouldn't worry about it."

Jake's face aches for more, but now is not the time to blurt out my darkest family secrets. Jake won't be able to handle it, and I definitely won't be able to handle it. Strategically, I change the subject.

"Let's get something to drink," I flirt, as I pull him toward the stairs.

Guiding Jake in front of me as we walk up the steps and over to the keg, I tap two cups of beer and look around for somewhere to sit. We end up squeezing ourselves on Mom's red couch in the corner, our backs against the wall.

Jakes hand rubs my thigh to reassure me, as I start to settle in. I glance across the room as one of Charlie's friends lights a cigarette. *Mom would kill this guy if she knew he was smoking in her house*. His hair is wildly out of control, and the dirt each strand is coated with is acting as some kind of hippie hairspray. He stumbles as he walks toward the front door and blows out a puff of smoke while the ashes float to the ground.

"Well, hello Mr. Kitty, how are you feeling tonight?" he asks, as he rubs his hand across the back of a ceramic cat Mom uses as a doorstop. "I bet you're puuuurrfect."

Jake and I point at each other, waiting to see who is going to break into laughter first as we watch Charlie's drunk friend continue to hold a conversation with a fake cat. I sit my empty cup on Jake's lap as I elbow him gently in the ribs.

"Can you refill my drink?" I ask, trying to sound like a damsel in distress. I wink at him as he glances at his still half-full cup. He chugs it down while I stand up and fix my shirt. "I'm gonna use the bathroom before it gets too gross."

Jake nods at me as he heads toward the kitchen to get refills. I stroll through Mom's office to the bathroom and turn on the light. The shower curtain is ripped from its hooks and Mom's beige rug is now stained with some sort of red liquid that I am praying isn't blood. I use the mirror to fix my hair when I hear a noise outside the door.

"Jake?" I ask, as I hear another rustle.

No answer. I shake my head and shut off the light while opening the door. Glancing into the laundry room, I see nothing but the hamper I used to hide in from Charlie when I was little. I close the door behind me and begin to walk into the darkness, changing my pace to more urgent rather than a casual stroll. Once into Mom's office, I hear a whisper pierce through the darkness.

"Where ya going, pretty lady?" it asks.

I stop; almost positive it is Jake playing a trick on me. However, something in my gut doesn't feel quite right. A hand brushes my neck, sweeping my hair to one side as his lips fold around my left ear. A nervous giggle escapes as his hands wrap around my biceps and spin me around to face him. The moon illuminates his skin; it isn't Jake.

"Don't make a noise!" he demands.

I nod as his fingers tighten around my arms and he pushes me to the ground. Stale cigarettes and alcohol escape his mouth as his breath blows wisps of hair from my eyes.

I pray someone will walk in. I hear voices just outside the door, but no one is responding to my silent pleas. He pushes his waist against my hips and reaches down to undo my belt. I close my eyes knowing not to scream, praying it will be over soon.

He twists my face towards him, shoving his tongue in my mouth. I choke down the vomit as I stare at Mom's computer screen hoping that if I can focus on anything else, this will fade in the background. His hand pushes down my pants as I wince in pain and try to count the seconds until it is over. As quickly as it began, the weight is lifted off me and the smell is gone.

"What the hell is wrong with you, you sick bastard?" Jake screams into the guy's face. "I ought to kill you right here."

I am safe now. A loud bang ricochets through the house as Jake slams the asshole against the wall and wraps his hands around his neck. Blubbering uncontrollably, I turn over to watch Jake scream at the guy as Charlie walks through the door, evaluating the situation. Curious partygoers have begun to cram into the entrance of Mom's office, trying to get a peek at the excitement.

"Your sister came on to me, man," the guy mumbles, obviously wasted. "I was hanging out and she just started kissing me."

Charlie glances at me as I struggle to stand up and buckle my pants. I wipe the tears from my eyes and cross my arms, so they stop shaking. I know we don't always see eye to eye, but I beg for him to believe that I didn't create this scenario. Setting his beer bottle down on the computer desk, he begins to walk toward Jake. His hand lifts from his side, his fingers waving in the air as he gets closer. Fear jolts me once again. I watch as Charlie's hand calmly falls onto Jake's shoulder and squeezes it to gain his attention.

"It's alright, man," Charlie says, calmly. "I got this."

Charlie asks Jake to step aside as he grabs the guy by his shirt and drags him outside. On the way out the door, Charlie points at me, "you stay right there, Sam," he instructs. "Jake, don't leave her alone again."

The doorway empties as the party parades out the front door behind Charlie. I'm not sure if I should be afraid or thankful for what he's about to do.

Jake wraps his arms around me and tries to calm my shaken bones as we wait for Charlie. When he finally enters, he refuses to make eye contact with either of us. Picking up his half empty beer off the desk, he is obviously winded as he struggles to breathe. Blood runs down his hands from his busted knuckles. After a sip of his beer, he brushes his hair from his face, and wipes the blood on his jeans.

"Sam, you and your boyfriend go up to your room and lock the door," he demands, as he takes another swig of beer. "I'll make sure no one else bothers you tonight."

“Thank you, Charlie,” I whisper.

“I would kill someone if they ever tried to hurt you, Sam. I thought you knew that.”

I didn’t know that. Apparently, Charlie’s rules don’t apply to himself. Maybe college changed him. Hopefully this is the start of a fresh relationship between us. I force a smile through drying tears as Jake wraps me in a blanket.

Charlie clears the way for us as his eyes make contact with any other guys at the party who may think of crossing boundaries.

It was the first time he has stood up for me since we were kids. A fleeting emotion takes over, convincing me that somewhere under there he still cares about me, or at least pretends to. I shoot a forced smile in his direction as I taste the saline from my tears in between my lips.

"Okay, Charlie," I nod.

Tightening my grip on Jake's hand, we walk up the steps. Once securely in my room, I lie on my bed and bend my knees to my chest. I pull the blankets up over me as Jake struggles to get the door to close behind him.

“Your brother seems like a pretty good guy,” he says. “He seems to really care about you, Sam. You’re lucky to have him.”

“Yeah,” I respond, unsure of what to say. One day I’ll share my past with Jake, but not today.

Peeling the contacts from my eyes, I watch his blurry arms pull his t-shirt over his head, and shove it under the crack in the door to block out the horror movie that is downstairs. Climbing into bed, his chest presses against me as I bury my face into his neck. Falling asleep in his arms, I realize that no matter how much someone loves me, I will never be safe.

Chapter 15

I watch Colleen as she bends over in front of Jake, wearing a disgustingly short skirt that just happens to show a hint of her lime-green thong. I gaze at Jake as he turns toward me, puts his finger in his mouth, and pretends to vomit. Colleen knows exactly how to push my buttons, but Jake always has a way to keep me from throwing her off of a cliff.

Colleen reminds me of little kid. She doesn't care what kind of attention she gets, as long as it's attention. It's like Jake is a toy, and she only wants him because I have him. She didn't want him when he was available before. Deciding I need some distance between us, I stand up and allow my hair to cascade in front of my eyes while reaching for Jake's hand.

"Wanna go somewhere away from everyone else?" I whisper in his right ear, while softly blowing on his neck. Lowering my hips onto his lap, I know it will help persuade him. He raises one eyebrow and contemplates the question. Breathing in the final drag of his cigarette, he flicks it into the woods and pushes himself out of the seat. Jill whistles in the background as we walk through the front door.

I peek back at Jake to make sure he isn't chickening out, before pulling him behind me as I climb the steps to the spare bedroom. At the top of landing, I turn my back to the wooden door and wait for Jake to reluctantly finish the steps. *Why isn't he more excited?*

Pulling his body into me, I clasp my hands together behind his neck and sink my lips into his. He lets out a small moan of disbelief as his hands fumble for a position on my lower back. Sliding my hand behind me, I turn the metal knob and force the door open. I put my finger to his lips, halting our kiss just for a moment, as I lead Jake into the darkness.

Floating to the bed, I take a seat. However, Jake isn't following. Halfway across the room he is sitting, motionless in the computer chair. I giggle at him, then cross one leg over the other acting confident, praying its enough to convince him I'm not absolutely terrified.

"What are ya doing all the way over there?" I say seductively, nervously awaiting his answer. *Why doesn't he want to sit by me? Does he not understand what's going on here? That he's finally getting laid after months of waiting?*

Jake's blue eyes cut through the dark room as they shift from the floor to my face. "Cuz I don't trust myself over there," he replies, shakily. It's the first time he's ever shown any insecurity. "I don't want to do something you aren't ready for. I don't know if I could stop myself. I mean, I know I could stop myself. I would never do something you didn't want. But it would be hard."

He's mumbling. I've never seen him like this and it's making me feel uneasy. I shake my head, motioning him to sit by me anyway. After he resists again, I stand up and make my way toward him. Once there, I rest my hands on his thighs. Whisking the chair around to face me, I lean down, grazing my cool lips on his cheek. His eyes roll in his head as he places his hands on top of mine.

"Okay," he whispers, locking eyes with me. "As long as you're sure."

Without a word, I pull him out of the chair and lead him to the bed in the corner. Lying back, I position him on top of me. My legs begin to tremble as Jake's hand coasts up my thigh, to its semi-permanent location alongside my hip.

"I'll crush you," he whispers, a worried look in his eyes.

I shake my head, and assist his hips down to meet mine, allowing his arms to release some of the weight they are struggling to support. Staring in my eyes, he brushes my bangs out of my face and runs his fingers down my chin, walking them across my collarbone. The heat of his body warms my core, and my entire lower region begins to tingle.

His weight shifts as he lowers his face down and his warm breath awakens my dormant mouth. I lift my head off the bed as I connect my lips with his and they become one. Simultaneously, I coast my trembling hands down his stomach and to his belt. My fingers freeze on his buckle. Jake halts his kiss and stares me in the eyes. I lower my head back down to the bed.

"You know, I love you, Sam," he says, seriously.

A rush of heat hurls through my body, and the room begins to shrink around me. I lunge my lips back up to his and caress my hands under his shirt. Each tense muscle in his back quivers as I graze over it.

This moment is so perfect, exactly how I dreamt it to be. My hands work to pull Jake's shirt over his head and throw it on the ground as he patiently awaits a response.

"I love you too, Jake," I whisper.

Supporting himself on one arm, he lifts me into a hug. As I breathe in the scent of his cologne, he softly returns me to the sheets. I hike my hips up toward him, bending my knees and allowing him to rest on top of me. A slight moan sneaks out to let him know I'm ready. Slowly, he slides his right hand up the small of my back and under my bra. His soft kisses sneak down my neck to the middle of my breast. This will be the first time anyone besides me has seen my boobs, and I'm feeling very insecure.

The clasp is undone with remarkable speed, and Jake begins to peel my shirt up my back and over my head. Suddenly, the confidence begins to dwindle as the insecurities rear their ugly heads. I silently worry whether he will be attracted or disgusted by my naked body; how badly it is going to hurt; if he will break up with me after he gets what he wants. Millions of thoughts are soaring around my mind. I'm so lost in fear that I am almost oblivious to the fact that Jake has begun to slide his hand up my skirt and pull down my underwear.

I am no where near ready for this like I thought.

"You okay, Sam?" Jake asks, sensing my change in mood.

Staring into his worried face I owe it to him to be honest, as awful as it may end up.

"I can't do this, Jake," I say, as I begin to push him off me, and pull my shirt back down over my chest. "I'm not ready; I'm sorry"

I feel the rest of his weight roll off me as he lets out a noticeable sigh of disappointment. There is a painful lump of guilt in my throat, like I swallowed a baseball covered in needles. My eyes scrutinize the back of his head trying to open it to see his thoughts as I fix my underwear. I stare at him while he sits miles away at the edge of the bed and rubs his face, so obviously frustrated. I await a response, begging for him to say anything—praying he will come lay with me and somehow understand. The bed squeaks as he stands up, reaches to the floor for his shirt, and begins to walk away.

"We better get back downstairs," he mumbles as his combs his hair out of his face. "We don't need them to come looking for us."

Jake's eyes refuse to look in my direction as he takes his first step toward the door.

I allow the tears to form as I hook the clasp on my bra and return my underwear to its position. Jake is out of the room before I can even say another word. I hear his footsteps down the stairs and out the front door. The engine of his car roars in the background before tires squeal out of the parking lot. So many emotions angrily flock into my head as I ridicule myself in the mirror. There are no bruises and no cuts, but I still feel like I just got the shit kicked out of me.

Jake is gone by the time I compose myself enough to make it down the steps. For the first time in our friendship, Colleen is silent when I pass her on the porch and make my way to the truck. As I slip the key in the ignition, I catch a glimpse from the corner of my eye of Jill running over to the passenger's side window.

"Picking me up at 10, right?" she asks through the glass. "I want a nice weekend," she adds as she watches the tears roll down my cheeks. Realizing my sadness, she allows sympathy to override her excitement. "You need this, Sam. Maybe some distance will be good for you both."

I nod my head and cover my eyes with sunglasses before Jill can say another word. Backing out of the driveway, I contemplate what text to send to Jake to fix this—if I can fix this. After a long ride home, and a lack of phone call from Jake, I decide to just let it be. We both need some time to figure out what we want, or at least I do.

Chapter 16

The seagulls squawk overhead as the sun burns through my abnormally pasty skin. Jill rolls onto her back next to me as she fixes her top and sprays another coat of lotion onto her arms.

"Let's go in the ocean," she whines. "I'm melting just laying here."

Colleen called this morning to say she couldn't come, and Jill has been in a rotten mood ever since. Thankfully, her cousin Bailey decided to ride along with us last minute to help foot the bill of gas. The two-hour drive to the beach was a headache, and now that we are finally here, all Jill wants to do is go home and ream out Colleen for bailing on us. I reluctantly stand up, brushing the sand off my thighs.

"You coming, Bailey?" I ask, rudely interrupted by the sound of Jill's impatient grumbling in the background.

Bailey lifts her face out of her book and smiles at me. Her short brown hair is pushed back off her forehead with a red polka dot headband. Her green one-piece bathing suit hides beneath a plus-sized robe that masks her overweight frame. Her nose scrunches to block the late afternoon sun, as she peeks out from under the umbrella.

"No, thanks," she mutters, and then quickly returns to her book.

I smile, "Maybe next time," and reluctantly follow Jill to the water.

"So, what's the deal with Bailey?" I ask, as I push through the knee-high waves. "How come you never invited her to hangout with us before?"

Jill snorts as she tries to figure out if I am being serious or sarcastic. After realizing I am genuinely intrigued, she fills me in on the details.

"Bailey is weird," Jill starts as her hand grazes the top of the sparkling water. "Her house is so small, and it smells gross, and although my aunt is the sweetest woman in the world, she and Bailey's dad don't have the greatest relationship," she continues. "We kind of only associate with them at family events, because anything more than that is torture."

Jill's statement is halted by a wave that smacks her in the back throwing her off balance. "She's nice," she adds, as she regains her composure, "but I don't know ... there's just so much about her I don't understand. We are just from completely different worlds."

I can't help but find a common connection with this stranger. From what I gathered, Bailey seems a lot like me. Her home life might even be almost as dysfunctional as mine. Besides, after this last straw with Colleen, I might be in the market for a new friend soon, anyway.

The saltwater fights with me as I struggle to exit and make my way back to our beach chairs. Grabbing a seat next to Bailey, I spark up a conversation.

"So, where do you live?" I ask, as I wrap a towel around my shoulders.

Bailey finishes reading her page before folding the corner down and closing her book. She wrinkles her forehead at me, wondering why I am suddenly intrigued.

"On a farm," she begins, "there's a lake out front. Sometimes I sit on my porch at night and listen to the bullfrogs and read," she continues, as her eyes begin to light up. "It's beautiful, Sam. You like to fish?" she asks, as she nods her head in my direction, "there's some real big fish in there." Her hands rise in front of her about a foot apart from each other, demonstrating the size of the fish in her pond. I listen in awe as she finishes up. "You could come over sometime, you know? I mean, if you want. I would love to have someone to go fishing with."

She's a little awkward and talks faster than any person I know. When she gets excited, her hands wave like an old Italian grandmother. She has this strange thing that she does with her fingers whenever she ends a sentence, as if she is flicking some imaginary ball into the air, but I can't help how strangely interested I am in every word that flows from her mouth.

"That sounds like fun," I blurt out.

Jill returns with a questionable look on her face as she lies down on her stomach and unties her bikini top. Flipping her hair to the side, she flicks the screen on her cell phone and begins to text Colleen for the millionth time today.

"I can't wait to go home later," she tells us, as she throws her phone in her purse. "We are heading straight to Colleen's so I can see what the hell her problem is."

--

Jill's new wave of anger is making me uncomfortable. I sing along to the radio on the way home to fill the awkwardness that has taken over the sedan as Jill rants, and Bailey shoves her nose in some book. Jill's headlights cut through the blackness of the summer night as we pull into Colleen's driveway.

Just as she's about to snap off the headlights, I notice the shine of a black convertible sitting in front of the garage.

"What's Jake doing here, Sam?" Jill asks, as her head turns toward me. "Did you know he was meeting us here?"

I shake my head as I pull my phone out of my purse to check for a text from him that I may have missed, but nothing. I suddenly realize that I haven't spoken to him since yesterday when he stormed out. I unhook my seatbelt and follow Jill to the front door. She bolts through it without knocking. I remain lost in her shadow, struggling to keep up with her through the living room, until she comes to a screeching halt outside of Colleen's bedroom door.

Jill spins the knob, but it's locked. Now enraged, she slams on the door with her fist and repeatedly yells Colleen's name. I slowly slide my body along the living room wall; far enough away to keep me safe from the violence that may unfold when Colleen's door finally swings open.

With my ear pressed against the drywall, I hear Colleen scurrying around her bedroom. Moments later, the knob spins and the door is opened just enough for Colleen to sneak out of the darkness. As she wipes her eyes and steps into the lighted room, I take notice of her pink bra strap hanging off her shoulder out from under her twisted t-shirt. After zipping the crotch of her jeans, she bends over and wraps her hair into a messy bun on top of her head.

"What's your problem, Jill?" Colleen asks, as she rolls her eyes and pushes past her. "Big deal I didn't go to the beach. Mom said I couldn't."

Their voices fade into the background as they move through the house screaming at each other. I hear a rustle come from the bedroom and creep forward to investigate.

Placing my left hand on Colleen's boy band poster, I slowly push the door the rest of the way open. My eyes halt once the light illuminates his figure, and ice freezes every muscle in my body. Unaware of my presence, he brushes back his hair while he struggles to find his boxers lost on the dark floor. My heart stops beating, and I can't breathe; I suddenly feel heavy. This is the hardest punch in the gut I've ever taken. The only person I've ever loved has ripped out my heart and smeared it across my friend's bed— then had sex all over it.

This isn't a mistake; all those times Jake told me he was repulsed by her were lies. I push down the hysterics that are beginning to escape as I run toward the front door. Struggling to find my car keys in the bottom of my beach bag, I collapse onto the gravel. Bailey's arms are the only things that stop my face from hitting the driveway, as she wraps them around me. The tiny rocks embed themselves into my kneecaps, but the pain doesn't even hold a candle to the emotions running through my head.

"Give me the keys, Sam," she demands, as she reaches out to lift my limp body from the ground. "I'll get you outta here."

I black out on the car ride. I am so tired of feeling my phone vibrate with text messages and phone calls that I shut it off. Bailey parks the truck on the side of a dirt road that I didn't know existed. Gazing out the window, I take notice of a wrought iron bench sitting on the bank of a lake.

"This is where I come on my worst days," Bailey says, as she turns off the car and hands me the keys. "I thought we could hang out here for a while."

I study Bailey's face as she awaits my response. Her eyes are so genuine and calm that they relax me. I watch her body stroll away as she exits the car and heads to the bench. I struggle to open the door and place my feet on solid ground. Putting one foot in front of the other, I hike my way to Bailey and stand behind her as she pats her hand on the metal seat.

"We don't have to talk if you don't want to," she says, staring out at the moonlit lake, "but I am a great listener."

I fake a smile at Bailey while pulling my knees in front of me and leaning my forehead on them. The bullfrogs bellow in the background and a light breeze dries the tears from my cheeks as I take a few deep breaths.

The fresh air casually reminds me of how beautiful things can be even on the ugliest of nights. I curl up next to Bailey on the bench as she lifts her arm around me and rubs my shoulder. Staring at the lily pads on the water, the moon reflects off the tiny waves.

"You know," Bailey whispers, "the days I feel really sad are the days I feel the most alive."

I lay my head on her shoulder as she pulls a cigarette from her purse and lights it.

“Want one?” she asks.

I accept her offer and take my first drag. The hot smoke burns my throat, and I cough it back out. Luckily, the smell is different than Jake’s, so I don’t have to sit and bask in his scent. I know that things will get harder before they get better, and I hope that Bailey will be there for me along the way.

I wave goodbye as I walk to my car and start the engine. Refusing a free ride, Bailey coasts barefooted down the road to her house as I illuminate her path with my headlights, making sure she arrives safely.

On the ride home I litter the roads with anything that reminds me of Jake. By the time my head hits the pillow I am so exhausted that I can't fumble through the lies anymore. Tonight, Charlie doesn’t scare me as I listen to his footsteps climb the stairs, there’s nothing left he can take away.

Chapter 17

I fight to open my eyes and shut off my ears from the annoying clicking of the keyboard across the room. Bailey shifts away from the dim-lit computer, squinting to see if I'm awake or not.

For the past three months, I have spent every waking moment at her house trying to escape from the rest of my life. However, our sleep schedules are polar opposites. Bailey is very much a morning person, and I am more of a vampire, making my way outside once the moon is the only thing in the sky. I roll away and take refuge under the sanctity of the down blanket keeping me warm, hoping Bailey will let me fall back into a sleep coma.

"Your phone went off a little while ago," Bailey whispers. "I didn't want to wake you, even though I have no idea how you sleep through that snoring," she snickers, simultaneously pushing me on the shoulder. "No wonder you can't find a man."

I grab a pillow from behind my head and throw it at Bailey's side; she grabs it and lets out a fake cry. I roll my eyes and smirk, undoing the French braid Bailey had in my hair.

"Very funny," I say, as I rub the sleep from my eyes, "you gonna shower sometime today, you bag of stink?"

I reach for my phone. Bailey sticks her tongue out at me while grabbing her cat-shaped mug filled with herbal tea. After taking a sip and swishing it around her mouth, she sets the mug back down and finishes her latest book review. Too lazy to reach for my glasses, I shove the screen to my face and allow my eyes to adjust, reading the black letters in my head. Then, I hand the phone the Bailey.

"It's from my mom," I say, with little emotion.

Bailey raises her eyebrows and shrugs her shoulders, waiting for more juicy details. When I don't respond, she reads the text.

"No way!" Bailey exclaims. "She wants you home for dinner so you can meet Charlie's new girlfriend?" she questions as she rolls her eyes. "Apparently, it's the big night of introducing her to the family. Well, don't you feel lucky?" Bailey sticks her finger in her mouth, quickly followed by a fabricated gag. "A girl would have to be crazy to willingly date Charlie," she adds, shaking her head in disbelief as she hands the phone back.

Even though she never met my brother, the stories I told her about him paint a pretty good picture. She's the only one I've ever shared my abusive childhood with— actually, it's the first time I've ever said it out loud, even to myself. I trust that she won't tell anyone and will keep my secret safe. If Mom or Charlie knew, I would be six feet under.

Spending close to five minutes waking up my muscles, I throw the blankets off and realize this day is coming, whether I like it or not. Staying at Bailey's isn't an option. I have to go home, and I'm not happy about it.

Pushing my sneakers on over blue and green toe socks, I wave goodbye to Bailey as I walk toward the door.

"I'm sure I'll be back in a few hours," I say as I toss my hood over sun-kissed waves of auburn hair. "Leave your door unlocked for me, ok?"

We both know that any 'family gathering' at my house has a good chance of turning ugly. Her door is always open— no questions asked.

Bailey smiles and grabs a towel out of the closet as she heads to the bathroom. "Always. Mi casa es su casa," she whispers, down the hallway.

I respond with a click and a wink while pulling the front door closed. The chill of the afternoon air slides down my neck as I start the ignition and pull a cigarette out of my pocket. Mom hates that I started smoking, which adds to the enjoyment of me doing it. I crack the window as I back down the dirt road and blow smoke out the window. The song on the radio stirs up old memories as I cruise toward home.

--

Wrapping my hand around the key to turn off the engine, I freeze for a moment. An idea of fleeing almost takes over before I twist the key and pull it out. I glare out my passenger-side window at Charlie's new truck, sitting there, gawking at me.

The shiny blue panels and crisp leather seats scream money. It doesn't take a rocket scientist to figure out that Mom and Dad co-signed the loan, but ignorance keeps me safe. It's not something I'm stupid enough to bring up. Charlie is the favorite and pouting about the unfairness isn't going to change anything. I glance in the window at the pink sweatshirt hung over the passenger seat and cringe at the idea of some girl finding Charlie *irresistible*.

Impossible to sneak in or out of this house, the plastic in the front door bangs as I close it.

Mom's voice springs through the living room, "Sam is that you?" she yells from the kitchen.

No, it's not me. Even though you just sent me a text thirty minutes ago, demanding I get home at once to awkwardly sit in on a dinner— with my asshole of a brother and his idiotic new girlfriend— so that you and Dad can pretend I belong in this family because we have company, and act as though you care about my opinion in front of her.

"Uh, yea Ma, it's me," I mumble in response.

My sneakers hit the heater vent when I kick them off on the mat. The zipper on my black-hooded sweatshirt doesn't go high enough to make me completely disappear, so I'm forced to continue through the house. The chatting voices warn me of what horrible fate lies beyond this seemingly safe position securely out of view. I suck a breath down into my tight lungs to relax my chest as I enter the tile floor and walk through the threshold to hell. Her incessant giggling makes my heart stop as I catch sight of French manicured nails running across Charlie's back.

"Hey, Sam," Colleen says, smiling, "long time no see."

She can't even manage to stop giggling long enough to get her words out. Blinking repeatedly doesn't change the fact that she is sitting in front of me— at my table— in my house. I feel like I've been punched in the throat, as heat flies up my body. It takes all I have not to wrap my arms around her neck and strangle her.

Don't do it, Sam. She's not worth sitting in jail for. Or maybe she is.

I haven't spoken a word to Colleen since the day she ripped my happiness from me and destroyed it. I have not forgiven her for sleeping with Jake and wasn't planning on ever changing my mind. If I never saw her bleached-blonde straw hair again, it would be too soon.

Charlie wraps his arm around Colleen's shoulder as she shifts her body closer. I gag as I slowly slide down into my seat across from her. She continues to smile as she scrutinizes me from the other side of the table, rubbing her hand on Charlie's leg.

"So, Colleen," Mom says, noticing the cloud of tension that has risen in the room, "tell me how you and Charlie met."

Her dark-lined eyes flutter in Charlie's direction. Lies cut out of her mouth so fast it is amazing she doesn't get lost in the web she creates. The entire table is hypnotized by her. I never understood the appeal, and I never will.

Scooping a helping of mashed potatoes on my plate and smothering it with gravy, I hope that food will keep me quiet.

"Well, I met him when Sam invited us to come over to a party, she was having here a few months ago," Colleen says as she locks eyes with me. "I think you guys were away for the weekend," she adds. She's challenging me; baiting me to cover my tracks from the party, but I'm not biting.

Dad's face is buried in the newspaper, mumbling on about baseball scores to Charlie, and luckily Mom is too busy picking out wedding china for the future married couple that the obvious lie Colleen is trying to set me up with goes right over their heads. Deciding I'm over this, I stand and begin to walk away. Unfortunately, her high-pitched voice grabs my attention.

"So, Sam," she says, getting me to pause and turn to her. "Charlie and I want to know if you want to go to dinner with us tomorrow night. You know, so us *old friends* could catch up?" she asks, with a smirk.

Her evil laugh coupled with the words 'old friends' sends a wave of anger through my body. My fists clench as I contemplate which one I should use to answer her question. Mom and Charlie stare at me as they nod their heads, motioning me to accept.

"I'd love to," I force through clenched teeth.

Refusing the chocolate cookies Colleen brought, I slip out the front door and into my truck before anymore discussion can unfold. My hands grip the steering wheel as I slam it from gear to gear. My temper is taking off, and for the first time, I can't seem to get it under control.

Parking on the road, I bust out of the cab and sprint to the front door, hoping Colleen will answer.

"Sam, is something wrong?" Charlie yells from the backyard. "Do you have a problem?"

Something in his eyes sets me straight without another word.

"No, I'm fine," I respond, heading back to the truck.

I can't lay a finger on Colleen, and she knows it. She saw how he protected me at the party that night, and now she's using it against me. Just when I think Charlie has my back, everything changes. Colleen has successfully ruined another budding relationship in my life, and there's not a damn thing I can do to stop it.

Chapter 18

Bailey's jaw drops to the floor when I tell her what happened. Even after all this time, stories about my family still shock her.

“Who needs television when you have the Mallon soap opera on 24/7?” she jokes.

“Dude, I should be selling this shit to a movie producer. I bet I could make millions,” I respond.

“You definitely can’t make this stuff up,” Bailey giggles as she heads into the kitchen for ice cream. “Want some?” she asks, grabbing a bowl from the cupboard.

“Sure,” I respond, plopping down on the worn couch. The scent of dog pee has me reevaluating, and I decide standing is a much better option. “I can get it,” I say, hurrying to the kitchen.

Scooping chocolate ice cream into my bowl and dousing it with whipped cream and rainbow sprinkles, I follow Bailey outside.

“So, what are you gonna do?” she asks, inquisitively.

“Well,” I mumble while licking my spoon. “I guess I’m going to put a smile on my face and go to dinner with my two mortal enemies.”

A bat dives down to scoop a drink of water from the lake.

“I guess you don’t have a choice,” Bailey whispers. “Perhaps, it’s a fresh start to the worst few months of your life.”

“I doubt it,” I murmur.

--

The next day is filled with panic attacks. Every moment, I force my mind to shut off so that I don't fret about the night to come, but it's practically impossible. My muscles ache as I shower, trembling under the lather from the loofah, begging for reprieve. An hour later, I stand out front of Bailey's house, lighting a new cigarette with the embers from the one I just finished. The nicotine doesn't seem to be doing anything to calm me down.

Charlie's truck barrels down the gravel driveway. Colleen stares at me with an awkward smile. Charlie waves me into the cab and I stomp my cigarette on the ground and slide into the backseat, securing my seatbelt into the holder.

"Hey, Sam," Colleen snickers, turning to me. Her eyes are surrounded with thick black liner, and beige shadow climbs all the way to her eyebrows, that are —of course—perfectly waxed. Her push-up bra accentuates the DD's that are falling out of her v-cut shirt. The faux fur lining her coat hood gently touches the spiral curls hanging from her up-do.

"Hey," I respond, blowing away the strands of hair that fell from my ponytail when I lowered my hood.

Charlie nods at me in the rearview mirror, and I wonder if our relationship is on the road to recovery. I smile, and then push my nose into a romance novel that Bailey lent me.

An early snow begins to fall as we travel unknown roads to the outskirts of town. After a half an hour of driving, we pull into a club that Colleen and I have no hopes of getting into.

"What is this place?" Colleen asks. "Charlie, I don't have my fake ID with me. I thought we were just going to dinner?"

Colleen fumbles through her purse with transparent insecurity.

"I'll wait in the car," I mumble.

“Don’t worry guys, I know the bouncer,” Charlie says as he pulls money out of his wallet. “That means you too, Sam. Get out of the car.”

I do as he says, and follow closely, watching Charlie hand a few select bills to the large man in a black t-shirt that reads “bouncer” across the chest. He gives a brief once-over and steps aside, allowing us to enter. Shoving the book in my waistband, and tossing the hood back over my head, I follow Colleen and Charlie inside.

The room is illuminated by black light as girls in bikinis dance on a stage to the left. Guys gawk at them from all angles, saying things like “bend over” and “shake it”. Steering clear of any signs that may say, ‘Amateur night’ I keep my eyes planted on the back of Colleen’s head, wondering if Jake ran his fingers through those blonde curls while he made love to her. I’d like to rip them out of her skull.

“Sit here,” Charlie instructs, “I’m gonna get us some drinks. You guys can order some food if you want. I’ll be right back.”

We take a seat at a high-top table with french fries littering the floor beneath it. I scoot forward on the bar stool as my sweater sticks to the back of it. Slightly disgusted, I grab a menu from the napkin holder and scan over it avoiding any eye contact with the blonde-bitch sitting across from me.

“What do you wanna get to eat?” Colleen asks.

I ignore her, shifting the menu in front of my face, making it very clear that I have no interest in making conversation.

"You know, I didn’t mean to hurt you, Sam," she says, placing her right hand on top of mine. "Jake and I were just something that happened in the moment," she continues as our eyes lock. "I'm sorry I did that to you, but I can't change it."

I yank my hand away and rub her disgusting apology off on my jeans. The lack of empathy makes it obvious that Charlie forced her into it.

"You know what Collee, F—."

Before I can get the words out, our conversation is interrupted by a duo of young guys. Two handsome blonde strangers with dark-tan skin and gorgeous blue eyes take a seat at our table, and I'm not complaining.

"Hey, ladies."

Flipping the hood off my head, I pull the hair tie from my ponytail and allow it to fall. I have a point to prove to Colleen, and these guys are the perfect way to do that.

"Hey," I respond. "I'm Sam."

"And I'm Charlie.:"

A strong whiff of tequila hits me like a baseball bat. With his hands on both their shoulders, Charlie redirects our surfer boys to a nearby table full of college girls.

"These are more your speed," he says. "Get my drift?"

The guys nod their heads, "Sorry, bro. Our mistake."

With the wave of his hand, Charlie directs us out of the bar. "Time to go, Sam. Get in the car."

I quickly jump off the bar stool and hurry to the car, struggling to keep stride with Charlie. He holds Colleen by the bicep, shoving her in front of him, hurrying her pace. She battles with him in the parking lot, attempting to rip her arm from his grasp, but with every struggle, his grip tightens.

Well aware of his temper, I stay in the shadow, strategically out of his direct view. I hope Colleen keeps her mouth shut, or we are both in for a long ride home.

The ticking of my watch is the only noise in the car for an agonizing fifteen minutes. I scoot down in the seat, hoping to make myself invisible to the fight I know is about to occur. Staring out the window, I watch the white line move back and forth as alcohol takes over Charlie's system. He jerks the wheel repeatedly, struggling to stay on the road.

Soon enough, his enraged voice shatters the silence.

"So, I guess you just thought it was a good idea to wear a low-cut shirt tonight!" he yells through the cab of the truck, "and just have all the guys come over and want to take you home; to have them think you are just open for business or something."

I look down at my turtleneck sweater. *What is he talking about, low-cut shirt?* Colleen's voice cracks with fear as she responds to his rhetorical questions.

"Stop being jealous," she tells him as her voice shakes. "I didn't ask those guys to come to our table, and before you came in acting all territorial, I was about to tell them to leave. I can wear whatever I damn well please!"

Just as Charlie begins to digest her words, she spouts out again.

"Why don't you get your facts straight before you go accusing me of stuff? It's not my fault you are insecure!"

I am so used to Charlie always directing his anger at me, that the thought of him yelling at Colleen catches me off guard. My focus shifts from the white line to Charlie's eyes, they are glazed red and locked on Colleen's face.

"What do you mean, insecure?" Charlie screams, "You are MINE; no one is going to change that!"

His hands grip the steering wheel as they imprint onto the leather and the truck begins to slow. I telepathically beg Colleen to stop challenging him, but she isn't budging. Her eyes have found safety in her cell phone, ignoring Charlie's threats, yet unknowingly egging him on.

You never ignore Charlie. The only hopeful solution to his rage is to agree with him and leave it at that. It is a tightrope to walk, and I watch as Colleen is beginning to lose her balance.

"Whatever, Charlie," she says, rolling her eyes. "You don't own me." Colleen's hand lifts in front of her face in Charlie's direction, directing him to shut up.

My hands instinctively rise to protect my face as I await Charlie's fist to connect with it. Peeking through the cracks in my fingers, I scan the steering wheel searching for Charlie's hands. Just as I locate them, his right one lifts and shoots like a bullet toward the passenger seat. Colleen scurries away, clinging to the door, pulling the handle trying to open it.

He misses.

Charlie struggles to keep the wheel straight with his left hand. "You're a slut. You stupid whore!" he screams. After steadying the wheel again, he jabs his fist toward her for a second time. This time, it connects with her temple.

I shut my eyes, unable to watch anymore as the sounds of fists hitting bone echo through the cab of the truck.

"Charlie, no!" Colleen screams from the front seat.

I force my eyes open and notice a small cut has now formed above her brow where Charlie made contact. I watch as the blood trickles down her forehead and onto her cheek.

I pray for it to end, but it's only the beginning.

His fist shoots toward her again.

Struggling for protection, her arms flail in front of her forming a small wall. Her cell phone falls to the floor as she turns her back to him and curls up against the window.

"Sam! Please help me!" she screams continuously.

I am frozen. The fear of Charlie's fists are keeps me from helping her. Being Charlie's punching bag for a good portion of my childhood has ruined me. There's no way I am going to sacrifice myself to protect Colleen. Not after what she did to me. She doesn't deserve Charlie's wrath, but neither do I.

The blood-curdling screams echo again as I watch Charlie's hand tighten around her mess of blonde curls. His forearm muscle flexes as he pulls back, pointing Colleen's chin to the roof of the truck.

Like a rocket, her face plummets down toward the dashboard. The sound of her skull hitting the plastic is deafening. My eyes beg to stay open, but the fear forces them closed once again.

Through the cracks between my fingers, I gaze at her motionless body, hunched over in the seat. Her face is pressed against the dash, lying in a small pool of blood.

Charlie's eyes shift from Colleen to the review mirror, searching for me. I remove my sweaty hands from my face and connect sights with him expecting it to be my turn. Charlie lifts his pointer finger in front of his mouth and puckers his lips.

"Shhhhhh," he whispers. "Not a word, Sam."

I nod, agreeing to his request.

Colleen's limp body hangs on the dash as Charlie continues to struggle to keep the car on the road. Agonizing minutes tick by until she begins to shake and rests her head against the side window for support. Charlie leans over and opens the glove box, pulling a tissue from the darkness as he begins to Colleen what happened.

"You ok, baby?" he asks, concern coating his words. "Here's a tissue. We were arguing about the guys at the bar, and you got yourself so worked up that you must've passed out and slammed your head off the dashboard."

He wipes blood-soaked hair from her face, and then glances in the rearview mirror.

"Sam and I didn't' know what was going on," he finishes, staring back at me. "Have you ever fainted before?"

Colleen is incoherent as she works to regain consciousness. I put my hand on her right shoulder while Charlie reaches to calm her shaking legs.

"I don't' think you need to go to the hospital," he says as he rubs her, "I'm sure you will be just fine."

I slam my hips against the seat as I fall backwards with disbelief. *Did Charlie do this for me? Did he know that Colleen slept with Jake, and ruined my life? It's a heavy price to pay, and I don't want to be a part of this revenge. Or, do I?* I definitely did not want to see Colleen get hurt, but knowing that Charlie wasn't really interested in her, and was doing it as revenge is slightly refreshing. Maybe his plan was to dump her when she started to care about him? Maybe he was going to hurt her like she hurt me, and then his temper took over?

Yet, here we are. I know Colleen needs to go to the hospital; she is not ok. I pull my phone from my pocket and dial 9-1-1 across the screen. My finger shakes as it hovers over the call button, wondering if I'm doing the right thing.

"Ok sis, here's your stop," Charlie says, as he puts the truck in park and flicks on the interior light. "Why don't you put your phone away? I have everything under control. You don't want to do something you'll regret, Sam."

I am so lost in the severity of the night that I didn't realize how close we were to Bailey's house. I glance at Colleen as she forces a smile in my direction, lifting her hand to wave goodnight. "I'll be fine, Sam," she forces out. "Let's do dinner another night, ok? We could catch up."

Charlie smiles as I exit the truck. Deleting the number off my screen, I shove the phone back in my pocket and light a cigarette. Charlie nods in approval as I thank him for a wonderful night and close the door to his truck.

My heart sinks as I watch Colleen's head fall while Charlie backs out of the driveway. Guilt overcomes me, knowing I am partially responsible, yet powerless. My only hope is that Charlie drops her home, and she never sees him again. Hopefully she will see a doctor in the morning, and the blows to her head cause no lasting issues.

I walk the deck steps to the wooden porch swing overlooking the lake and take a seat. The chains squeak as I swing my feet back and forth, staring at the light flakes of snow, begging for some kind of solution to this. To save Colleen, I would've had to sacrifice myself. I would've felt the force of Charlie's fist once again, and that's something I'm not willing to do. We've made some progress these past few months, even if it was baby steps. Fighting with my conscience, I battle with my heart. I wish someone would've saved me from Charlie all those years ago, but I'm not sure I'm the one who can do the saving this time.

I watch the lake as the snow becomes heavier, making tiny ripples on the surface. I study how much effect one little ripple has on everything in its path until it crashes into land.

Walking to the edge of the water, I toss a few pebbles in, trying to get the tiny waves to speak to me, hoping they will tell me something. After several hours, my windburn cheeks and frozen feet beg me to the warmth inside.

Bailey is asleep when I shuffle in. I stare at her from the computer chair as I seriously contemplate waking her up, desperately needing advice. Ultimately deciding against it, I curl up beside her in bed.

My sleepless night is filled with trying to decipher how I am going to break the cycle. I wonder how a small piece of land like me, could stop the gigantic ripple of Charlie.

Chapter 19

A loud knocking on the front door rips me out of my morning slumber. I chose to sleep here last night instead of Bailey's because I longed for a home-cooked meal. Bailey's family lives off of fast food and it's wreaking havoc on my stomach. I hear Mom shuffle from her bedroom and barrel down the steps to see who could possibly be knocking so early. The knob turns and the door creaks open.

"Hello, Ma'am," a man says, "I'm Officer Jordan. I am wondering if I could have a few words with your son, Charles?"

I crawl out of bed and sneak toward the door. Lying on the plush pink carpet, I press my face against the crack to see down the steps. Mom pulls her robe tight, and waivers back and forth on her blue slippers. Her left-hand rests on her face while her right arm wraps around her stomach.

"What is this about?" she asks.

"There has been a report of domestic violence made against your son, Charles Mallon, and we need to look into it," the officer states as he removes his sunglasses, folds them, and places them on his wooden clipboard.

Before Mom can answer, Charlie exits his bedroom and slowly begins down the steps. Ending in the foyer, he towers over the small man in uniform.

"I'm Charles Mallon, sir," he says, standing confidently still, crossing both arms in front of his chest. "I would like you to read me the charges, and please tell me who filed them. I know my rights."

The officer pulls his reading glasses out of his shirt pocket and rests them on the bridge of his nose. Lifting the top page of his notes, he begins to read the paperwork.

"There are currently several charges pressed against you for domestic violence, simple assault, and harassment. There was a report made at County Hospital three weeks ago when a young woman came in with a severe headache, blurred vision, and a fractured nose."

The officer pauses and glances up at Charlie, observing his reaction.

Charlie stands poised, completely unfazed.

The officer continues, "When questioned about the injuries, she stated that you told her she passed out and banged her head off the dashboard. The state believes that violence has been a possible part of this and it is our job to investigate further. We would like to ask you a few questions about that night."

The officer finishes and nods his head at Charlie for approval. I swallow down the lump in my throat as I struggle to breathe quiet enough to remain unheard.

"Absolutely, Officer; I have no problem answering any questions you may have," Charlie says, as he unfolds his arms and relaxes them at his sides. "It seems that Colleen may have some amnesia from that night and is slightly confused, which I completely understand."

The officer nods his head and clicks the end of his pen, ready to record Charlie's testimony. After a momentary silence, he begins telling the officer his fabricated story.

"I took Colleen out for a nice dinner at a local restaurant. She had been up late the night before studying for an exam and said she needed to blow off some steam," Charlie continues, his eyes locked with the officer's gaze. "She always puts so much pressure on herself to do well in school. I thought a night out would help her relax. I didn't notice she was taking sips out of my drink every time I wasn't looking."

I move my hand across my mouth, fearing I might scream the truth down the stairwell. Shoving my ear against the crack, I realize it's too hard to hear and watch at the same time. I know I need to pay attention and memorize this story; if the cop questions me next, our facts *have* to match.

"Ok, Charles, what happened after you left the restaurant that night?" the officer asks, raising his eyes from his pad, hoping to catch Charlie struggling to answer.

My sweat-soaked hands cling to the carpet beneath me squeezing the fibers between my fingers. *Come on, Charlie. Think of something to get us out of this. I can't lie for you.*

"Colleen was very tired and started to drift off. I smelled the liquor on her breath and decided to take her home and let her get some sleep," Charlie says, as his eyebrows lift with sympathy. "I tried rubbing her leg to wake her up and have her put her seatbelt on, but she just kept drifting off. The roads were icy, and I was worried about getting into an accident."

He halts for a moment as the officer lifts the pen and bites the end of it, seemingly struck by the words 'accident.'

"Can you explain what happened to Miss Jones when she sustained the injuries we stated earlier?" the officer asks.

This is where I know Charlie will crack. There is no way he has this entire story planned out; no way he can answer these questions on the spot and make it sound believable. Sweat drips down my forehead and burns as it enters the corner of my eye.

"Of course," Charlie responds. "I was concentrating so much on the slippery roads that I hadn't noticed Colleen fall asleep. As soon as I started to lose control of my truck and slam on the brakes, I reached my arm across to protect Colleen, but I was too late, and her head smashed off the dash."

Charlie covers his eyes with his hand, and then continues as he shakes his head back and forth. "I got the truck to a stop and Colleen was passed out. I thought maybe she had fallen back asleep, but I was pretty sure she had hit her head. Seconds later, she woke up confused."

He pauses, looks from the officer to Mom, and then continues, "I dug a tissue out of the glove box for her bloody nose, and small cut she had above her temple. With only the dim interior light, I tried to examine her head and neck for any bumps or cuts as best I could. Nothing seemed too severe, but still I was concerned."

Charlie crosses his arms as he shrugs his shoulders, acting upset by the story. "We argued for about 10 minutes because I wanted to take her to the hospital, but she demanded we go home because she didn't want to get in trouble for underage drinking."

Charlie finishes as a single tear rolls down his cheek, "I should've just taken her, I know, but she told me she was ok. I trusted her judgement."

It is the perfect story; Charlie told it with such confidence that there could be no question to its validity. I'm impressed at his ability to lie to a man in uniform and, at the same time, terrified to the bone.

The officer places his hand on Charlie's shoulder. "Thank you, Charles, for your testimony. We will take care of this," he says, as he nods his head and winks at Charlie before turning and walking down the steps. "I'm sorry for the trouble," he apologizes with a wave of his hand.

I unknowingly let out a deep breath of air so loud that Mom turns and glances up the steps toward my room. Just as she begins to close the door, Officer

Jordan halts on the second-to-last step, motionless for a split second. Jerking his head and spinning on his heels, he quickly bounds back up the porch.

"One more quick question," he says through the small crack in the door, "Was there anyone else in the car with you the night of the accident?"

Charlie stands silently; it's the first question he seems unprepared for. My mind races as I wait for his answer. Horrible situations are parading off my skull at the speed of light. *What will I say if he questions me? What if I get the story wrong? What if I can't remember something?* Mom reaches out and places her hand on Charlie's chest before he can answer. Pushing him behind her, protecting him—protecting us—she begins to close the front door.

"No more questions until my son has a lawyer present. Thank you, officer. Good day," Mom says, as she pushes it shut and locks it.

I quickly scurry back to my bed. Lying in silence, staring at the ceiling, I watch the hours pass until it is late enough to justify coming out of my room without stirring up any skepticism.

I try to act as oblivious as possible as I walk into the kitchen, open the pantry, and pull out a box of cereal. Mom and Charlie are sitting at the table, staring at each other, as her hand grips the cordless phone.

"Sam, come sit down please," she says, motioning to the chair next to her.

A slight chill heads through my body as I pull out the chair and take a seat. Mom and Charlie stare back and forth at each other for what seems like hours, until they finally decide to throw the ball at me.

"Sam," Mom says, concern in her voice, "your brother is probably going to have to go to court to testify against Colleen in her crazy attempt to get him arrested for some bogus accusations of abuse."

I try to act shocked as she says it, but I'm sure my horrible attempts to be dramatic are incredibly transparent. I nod my head, letting her know I understand and urging her to continue.

"The lawyer says that there is a chance you may have to testify in front of the court about what happened that night," she states, nervously awaiting my response.

I freeze. My worst nightmare is laid in front of me, and I am about to dive into it head first. I'm aware that I have two options: I can testify for Charlie and stick to the story he told, lie under oath and risk the possibility of going to jail myself, or, I can tell the truth and risk the possibility of sending my brother to jail and losing my entire family. I wish there's an option three; I search for it, and I pray for it—but it doesn't exist.

Breaking from my thoughts, I listen as Mom and Charlie run through any loopholes that may exist in his story, making sure I know it word-for-word.

"This is the most important test you will ever take, Sam. You need to remember EXACTLY what to say. You need to protect this family."

Never did I expect to be protecting Charlie, or Mom, for that matter. These are the people who destroyed me physically and emotionally for the past 18 years. Then, as soon as they want something from me, I'm supposed to just do it, no questions asked. *But, what choice do I have?* If I don't do what they want, I'll be getting way more than a slap on the wrist. I kick myself for going to dinner that night; I should have listened to my instincts and just said no. However, trying to erase the past is pointless; it is the future that I need to expend my energy on.

"I'll say whatever you want me to say," I respond. "I will protect Charlie."

--

Bailey and I comb the internet for the details of domestic violence charges, sentencing, and the punishment for lying under oath. Nothing is helping; no decision is the right one. My phone vibrates in my pocket. I stop typing in the search engine just long enough to read it.

Mom:

Charlie's preliminary hearing is scheduled for December 5th at 8 am. Our lawyer wants to go over some things before then. Call me.

As I read the text aloud to Bailey, tears stream down my face. I have never been as afraid in my life as I am right now.

The frigid afternoon air smacks me in the face. Tiny flakes melt on my cheeks as I walk through them, hoping my anxiety will begin to fade. I know that the truth will set me free, but the need to protect Charlie is growing. Somewhere in my mind, I know he would protect me, and I should do the same for him.

--

The next morning, as I smoke a cigarette on the porch, the sun peeks over the mountains. Despite the chilly November air, the sunrise warms my skin and calms my soul. I study the shades of gold and amber as they inch their way into the sky, hoping with the new day, that the universe brings me some sort of answer.

Quietly, I take a deep breath and stare across the lake. The wind rips through the water, causing ripples to once again break the calm surface. As they travel across the darkness, a single island of land stops them before they reach the shore. I flick my cigarette onto the pavement and stand up to brush off my pants.

I finally know what I need to do; I am the island, and this is my chance to stop Charlie's waves.

Chapter 20

I am certain Charlie's face the morning of the preliminary hearing will forever be etched in my memory. His demeanor is stoic, yet his expression is condescending, laced with a cocky smile.

“So, now what?” Mom asks the lawyer as we stand in the entryway of the courthouse.

“Now, we go to trial. I’m pretty sure I can convince the judge to dismiss the case based on lack of evidence, though. So, I’m not too worried. But, if we do need to go to trial, I’m going to have to work with Samantha on witness prep. She needs to be firm on her story, and not let the prosecution get to her. They will try to break her, and it will severely damage our case,” George, our lawyer, states.

“I’m not worried,” Charlie smiles at me. “Sam and I know the truth. Everything will work out just fine, right sis?”

The pressure is so immense, that it feels like the weight of the world is resting on my shoulders. I haven’t been able to eat for days and have lost ten pounds. Vomiting has become a morning ritual, and panic attacks are a constant occurrence.

“Right,” I force out hoping Charlie doesn’t sense my uncertainty.

The lawyer hands over paperwork with a trial date before heading back into the court with another client. We pile into Mom’s car and head home, completely silent.

Once we arrive, the silence is broken when Charlie and Mom decide to celebrate prematurely.

"I can't believe that psycho actually thought she was going to put my son in jail," Mom says as she flips an egg in the frying pan, "Psychotic ex-girlfriends drive me nuts!" she adds as she whips around to the fridge and emerges with two slices of cheese.

Charlie loosens his tie, sweeps his hair to the side and smirks at Mom's banter. I feel completely out of place. If they only knew how I prayed all morning that the trial would end with Charlie being forced to get some sort of help for his anger. A sense of defeat rushes across my body when I look up to notice Charlie winking at me from across the kitchen as he rolls the cuffs of his dress shirt.

“You feel lucky, sis?" he asks as he rips out his ponytail, "to have a brother as amazing as this.”

His hand coasts the outline of his goatee before sliding down in front of his chest and shoving his thumb toward his sternum.

Not only does the sight of him nauseate me, but couple that with Mom drooling over his every move, and I’m finding it hard to hold down breakfast. Unable to finish, I push my bowl to the center of table just as the phone starts to ring.

"Mallon residence," Mom says as she lifts the phone to her ear. Her face changes from a rosy hue to a ghostly white as she listens to the voice on the other end of the line. Her mascara starts to run as tears begin to cascade down her cheek, yet no words are flowing from her mouth.

My disgust turns to worry. I push from my chair to rush to her side, but Charlie beats me there. He wraps his arms around her shoulders as she slowly places the phone back down in its cradle.

“That was the lawyer," she mumbles, fighting back the tears that are trying to creep out. "He said that new evidence has been brought to trial. Colleen apparently has witnesses from the club who state they saw you forcefully shoving her in the parking lot after drinking several shots inside. He also says two young men stated you were jealous when they came over to the table and acted controlling," she continues as she pushes her head into Charlie's chest for comfort. "He says if any of this is true, it could really disrupt our case. They are asking all of these people to testify against you in court."

Charlie and Mom both stare in my direction, pleading with me, knowing I'm their only hope. Charlie stiffens as he walks behind me and places both hands firmly on my shoulders, burrowing his thumbs into my spine. I freeze from the pain as his fingers dig deeper with every word out of his mouth.

"No worries, Mom," Charlie says, "Sam knows the truth. She said she will protect us, and she will."

Chapter 21

The courtroom is gray—not a nice gray, but more like a hospital gray— depressing and cold. The pantsuit I borrowed from Mom is too big and falls at the waist anytime I stand up. Behind the podium, where I assume the judge will sit, are oil paintings of gray-haired men, gawking at me— judging me. Large windows face the courtyard, where one lonely tree stands and waves as the wind blows through its branches.

Charlie sits in the corner chair with a confident smirk on his face, having no doubts that I am going to protect him and keep his secret, just like I always have. I stare at his fists as he cracks his knuckles and folds his hands on his lap. His hair is tied back into a slick bun, and his goatee is clean shaven. A black tie sits on his chest, neatly hanging down the button line of his, freshly pressed, blue dress shirt. His open fists now rest on his black slacks, staying out of trouble.

Our lawyer walks through the double doors and over to us with a concerned look on his weathered face.

"Colleen is outside," he says to Charlie, as Mom leans in to listen, "she brought the bartender from the club that night who is willing to testify that Colleen was 100-percent sober the night of the accident. Also, we found out it wasn't a nice restaurant that you guys went to; it was a strip club on the outskirts of town. Lying to me isn't helping your case, son."

He pauses, allowing the information to be digested, then continues as Mom and Charlie exchange glances. "If the prosecution convinces the jury that Charlie hurt Colleen that night, and that Charlie has been lying, he could go to jail."

Mom and Charlie murmur to each other, deciding the best route to take, as George turns to me, "And, Sam, if you lie for your brother, you'll be sitting in jail next to him."

I am drowning in all the sweat dripping from my pores. Anxiety attacks are destroying my life every two minutes and Charlie is just sitting there as if it was a normal day. Turmoil of anger begins to boil through my skin, knowing I'm risking my future to protect the secret, and he doesn't even care about the ramifications it could have on my life.

Mom turns her head, sensing my uneasiness, "You protect your brother, Sam, no matter what the cost. Blood is thicker than water. You have no allegiance to that girl. She destroyed your life."

I can't help but see Mom's point. Colleen never had my interests in mind when she slept with Jake. In fact, part of me believes it was her goal all along. She wanted to hurt me. Jake was something to win—like some kind of game. So, why am I even questioning taking her side?

My emotions summersault. My mind knows that if I don't tell the truth, then I'm just as guilty as Charlie, but my heart wonders what kind of sister testifies against her brother and sends him to jail?

Nostalgia takes over as I remember how much I used to love Charlie; all the memories we have together and how all of that could be destroyed after today. I know he will never forgive me if I go against his wishes. I listen to the lawyer as he whispers in my ear and rehearses my story with me for the last time. Sucking down the emotions, I ready myself to do what I need to do to keep Charlie safe; my big brother; my very best friend.

--

The courtroom doors open as family and friends shuffle inside and take their seats, filling in the empty wooden benches. I almost miss Colleen's entrance, as a wave of straight black hair— replacing her once bleached-blonde curls— heads down the aisle. Jill sits next to Colleen's mom, refusing to make eye contact with me as I smile in her direction. I still can't understand how she sided with Colleen in that whole thing, and I stopped trying to figure it out.

Moving my sights to the front of the courtroom, I examine Colleen as she whispers back and forth with her lawyer. Her tan suit fits perfectly; her well-groomed nails and hair makes her appear very trustworthy. I finally understand why Mom always says first impressions are so important. If I was the judge, I would choose her word over Charlie's, any day.

The last few people enter the courtroom as the officer asks everyone to please take their seats. My heart stops when I hear his voice behind me.

"Hey, Sam," he whispers.

I turn around in my seat just in time to see his giraffe body slide onto the bench.

"How you been?"

I ignore him. The last thing I need right now is Jake tugging at my heart. *What is he even doing here? Are him and Colleen dating now? Is he in love with her?*

I know I should be focusing on the trial, but I can't think about anything but Jake. A whiff of his cologne floats up my nostrils and tingles fly down my body. I forgot the way he made me feel. Luckily, the doors open, and the judge enters the court room before I'm forced to respond.

"All rise for Judge Gaglio," the officer says, interrupting me from the small suture being sewn on my broken heart.

A middle-aged salt-and-pepper-haired woman in a long black robe walks out from the door behind the stand. She spins her black-leather chair around and takes a seat. After scanning the courtroom, she slams the gavel, and we all follow her lead, taking our seats. Reading the charges against Charlie, she glances at the defendants and prosecution, explaining to each party what she expects out of the day. I listen intently as both Charlie and Colleen are called to the stand to testify, but I momentarily zone out, as my mind wonders about Jake again.

If he was here for Colleen, why wouldn't he sit with Jill and her mom? Why would he sit right behind me? I should've never blocked his phone number. Maybe he's been trying to contact me this whole time. I doubt it, if he really wanted to get in touch with me, he could've found me. Pay attention, Sam. Get a hold of yourself.

Pretending to care about the trial, I wait for Charlie to break as I study his body language after every question. He answers them perfectly. His voice doesn't waiver, and he never hesitates before responding. All the words flowing from his mouth are believable. With every answer, he manages to make Colleen appear like a crazy and irrational woman—just as he planned.

"No more questions, your honor," Colleen's lawyer says as he walks back over to his seat. "I would like to call my client, Colleen Jones, to the stand now, your honor," he adds.

Colleen rises from her seat and heads toward the chair confidently. Her heels click on the floor before coming to rest beneath her as she takes a seat at the podium. The microphone squeals as she drops it down closer to her mouth.

Her lawyer starts with a few warm-up questions about her age, and where she went to school, so the jury can get a sense of her personality and character. Finally, he asks her to replay the night of the accident.

"Charlie, his sister, Sam, and I all went out to eat at a bar that Sam and I were far too young to even get into," she starts as she keeps eye contact with her lawyer. "Charlie was drinking tequila shots at the bar while Sam and I took a seat at a bar table maybe twenty feet away. Two guys approached us a few minutes later and were flirting with us." She stops as she catches me in her sights. "Charlie saw the guys and came over, demanding that they leave. He then told us that it was time to go. He grabbed three more shots that he did on his way out the door." Colleen's lawyer nods his head as he listens to her story.

"Ok, Miss Jones, to the best of your recollection, can you tell me what happened next?" her lawyer asks, as he paces back and forth in front of her.

Colleen stares down at her hands for a moment before she begins.

"Well, we all got in the car, and no one really said much for a while. The roads were a little slippery and between the alcohol setting in and the weather, Charlie was having trouble keeping the truck on the road," she says nervously as her confidence begins to waiver. She takes a deep breath before she continues. "Charlie said something to me about the guys hitting on me at the bar, and how it was because of the low-cut shirt I was wearing. I told him to stop acting crazy and that he didn't control me. I remember his eyes were filled with anger after I said that, so I tried to focus on my phone instead of him. I don't remember much else after that."

As Colleen finishes, tears begin to form in her eyes. Her lawyer grabs a tissue from his pocket, hands it to his client, and then takes a seat.

Charlie's lawyer stands and brushes his comb-over to cover the one bald spot on his egghead, trying to make it less noticeable. I smile to myself when I notice it didn't work. He strolls to Colleen and stares at her, "Miss Jones," he says as he taps his fingers on his notepad, "Is it possible that you could have misinterpreted Charlie's concern for anger?"

Colleen shakes her head and wrinkles her eyebrows, "No, I don't think so."

"Has Mr. Mallon ever shown aggression to you before the night of this supposed incident?" he asks, strategically trying to falter Colleen.

"No sir, he hasn't," Colleen says as her eyes shift to the floor, and her hands fumble with one another under the desk.

Forgetting that her body is visible to the court, her one foot begins tapping on the carpeted floor as obvious nerves start to shine through her confident exterior.

"Well, then how can you be so sure that you didn't pass out and hit your head on the dashboard?" the lawyer asks, not really expecting an answer from Colleen at this point.

"Well ... I'm not positive. I don't remember what happened next," she replies.

Tears begin to run down Colleen's cheeks as she fights to remain calm. The lawyer turns to the jury.

"You're gonna believe the accusations of abuse from a woman who cannot recall what happened?" he asks the 12 men and women sitting off to the side. "No more questions, your honor."

Colleen is called down from the stand and asked to return to her seat. Her lawyer reassures her by placing his hand on her shoulder and whispering encouraging words in her ear.

“Are there any other witnesses that the prosecution would like to call to the stand?” Judge Gaglio inquires.

"Yes," Colleen’s lawyer responds confidently. “The prosecution would like to call Samantha Mallon to the stand please, your honor."

His voice echoes off the walls as he points across the courtroom toward me.

Jake's hand lands on my shoulder, and I freeze, "Good luck, Sam. I'm here for you."

It feels like a dream. Jake is throwing curveballs at me, and I'm not even up to bat. I have no way of dealing with that situation right now, so I shut down and focus on the task at hand.

Mom's warm breath brings me back to reality. "Stay strong, Sam," she whispers in my ear, "You can do this."

I slide passed her and into the aisle way, struggling to ignore the stares of the familiar faces lining the pews. Hiking my pants as I walk, my cheeks turn hot as I try to overcome the fear. Her lawyer stands in front of me, smirking with confidence. *Don't let this guy scare you; it's his job to trick you, Sam, you have to be smarter than him.*

"Miss Mallon, can you please rise and repeat after me?" the judge requests in my direction. The words resonate in my head as I repeat them: *promise to tell the truth.* Although I shutter inside, I speak loud and clear just as George had instructed.

The metal of the handcuffs on the officers guarding the door reflect the morning sunlight into my eyes, momentarily blinding me. Charlie smiles as he forms both hands into fists on top of the table. I shift my sights over to Colleen as she brushes hair out of her face and wipes underneath her eyes with a tissue.

And then, I see him.

Jake smiles at me from the back of the room. After all this time, there's no doubt that he still has my heart. I can't help it. If I would've been honest with him from the start about my childhood, there's a good chance we would still be together. I kept so much from him and there's still so much that he doesn't know. I don't forgive him for sleeping with Colleen, but I think I finally understand his reasoning. Everyone deserves forgiveness, even those who hurt us the most.

My eyes plead with him to save me; I want him to whisk me away from this and go back in time to that trampoline. Although I expect him to, he doesn't shift his eyes. For a split second in time, we are connected again. I taste his lips and long for his touch.

The brief reconnection is shattered when Colleen's lawyer repeats his question. I wipe my face with my hand and shift back into reality. "Miss Mallon, can you please recount the events on the night of October 8th?"

Mom nods her head as she holds Dad's hand in her lap. Her free hand rests on her knee, her rings pointing toward the ceiling. I look away from my family to Colleen, who rubs her forehead as she tries not to let the sense of defeat overcome her. She must know I despise her for what she did to me, and in about two minutes, I am going to completely throw her under the bus. I remain silent, waiting for someone else to answer the question for me, even though I know that it's not going to happen.

Then, like a shot in the dark, it hits me. This isn't Colleen's battle to win; it's mine. I have spent 18 years of my life living in fear. I have no voice, no choices, and no world outside what Mom and Charlie have allowed me to live. Even though he hasn't touched me in years, Charlie's only manipulating me to believe he cares. I am his pawn, and he's controlled every aspect of my life— including today.

I lost Jake because of him, and two of my best friends. I'm risking jail time to protect him, and yet he has absolutely no remorse. He doesn't care about me; no one in my family cares about me. *You need to get that statement through your head, Sam.* They have molded me over the years to be a pawn in their twisted game, scaring me into following their rules and keeping their secrets.

But I'm not afraid anymore.

The only way I can assure my safety, is to get Charlie the help he needs, and the only way to do that is with the truth. The words start to pour from my mouth, like a stream of water putting out a wildfire.

A heavy silence overtakes the courtroom as I finish my recollection of the night. Colleen's face is horrifying when she hears the truth of what happened to her. She feels the back of her head where Charlie ripped her hair before slamming her face down on the dash. As she runs her fingers across the small bald area, her jaw drops. Nothing could have prepared her for the truth, and I feel guilty throwing it at her, completely unfiltered.

The judge turns to me and stares into my eyes, evaluating my words for validity. Rivers of tears fall, washing away the silence I have kept bottled inside since I was a child.

The courtroom erupts with so many whispering voices that I can't figure out which ones are important. The judge slams her gavel against the podium, "Order in the court, please! Order in the court! Everyone take a seat, now!"

"No further questions, your honor," Colleen's lawyer states while handing me a tissue. "Thank you for your testimony, Samantha. You may have a seat."

I refuse to make eye contact with Mom or Charlie as I walk past them toward the back of the room. Jake switches his seat to join me. Allowing my head to rest on his shoulder, he wraps his arms around me and pulls me close. I silently sob. *What did I just do?*

--

An hour later, I listen as the judge reads the jury's decision aloud.

"In the case of Mr. Charles Mallon against Miss Colleen Jones, how does the jury find the defendant?"

A young woman stands from the first seat of the jury box, unfolding the paper in her hand. "On the charges of simple assault, and harassment, we find the defendant, guilty."

Applause flies from Colleen's family as they rejoice. Mom sobs uncontrollably, throwing herself into Dad's arms.

"I'm sentencing Mr. Mallon to six months' time and six months' probation. Mr. Mallon will also need to participate in anger management classes for a time determined by a licensed therapist, but no less than six months." She ends by motioning the standing officer to place Charlie in cuffs and escort him out.

I am flooded with guilt as I begin to regret what I've done. Charlie turns to look back at me as he walks through the doors, a police officer's hand holding the crook in Charlie's elbow. I expect to see fire igniting in his eyes, but instead, they are warm as they well up with tears. He mouths the words "I'm sorry," in my direction before turning back to face the officer.

There he is—my brother. I knew he was in there somewhere.

Chapter 22

Two days pass before Charlie is home again.

Due to overcrowding, his punishment has shifted to one year's probation, coupled with the anger management courses. I lock my door when I hear Mom's car pull into the garage.

The house has been a frigid environment since the trial, so I'm a little unsure of what will happen now. I shake under my sheets as I hear their voices carry up the stairs.

"So, what are you going to say to your sister?" Mom asks Charlie, pausing at the foot of the steps, barely in earshot.

I crawl out of bed and push against the crack under the door, awaiting Charlie's answer.

"I dunno, Ma. I just wanna go lay down for a bit," Charlie mumbles, as I hear him place his feet on the steps. "It's been a rough couple of days."

I run to the closet where I hide in the darkness behind Mom's suitcases, waiting for Charlie to knock down my door at any moment as I stare at the metal zipper on the luggage.

The silence is broken by the slam of his bedroom door. Footsteps journey across the wood floor of his room, and then the mattress groans out an audible squeak as he falls onto it. Confused by his behavior, I pull my phone from my jean pocket and call Bailey for insight.

"Do you think maybe you should move out of your mom's?" she asks, nervously.

"Yes," I whisper. "The sooner, the better."

Bailey invites me over to devise a plan. I hang up the phone and push the suitcases off of me as I muster the courage to sneak out of my room and down the stairs. Somehow while I was on the phone with Bailey, Charlie has managed to silently make it down the steps and into the kitchen. I try to scurry passed him and Mom quickly without any confrontation.

"Hey, Sam, where you going?" Charlie asks, his tone sending chills down my spine.

"I'm going over to Bailey's for the day; we talked about going snow tubing with some friends," I say, as confidently as possible.

Charlie's left eyebrow raises, questioning my answer. He scoops a heaping spoonful of corn cereal into his mouth as he continues to read the newspaper.

"I thought maybe you would want to go out with your big brother for lunch today?" he asks, his eyes shifting from the sports section to my face.

I force a fake smile in his direction, but I know he can see right through me. His eyes burn, trying to rip me down, waiting for me to beg for his forgiveness—a forgiveness that I'm not asking for and he's not giving. He places his spoon back in the bowl, and lays the paper on the table before standing and walking toward me. I watch his fists remain motionless by his hips as he inches closer. Pressing my back against the screen door, I feel the cold seep through my jacket.

For the first time ever, I challenge Charlie with my eyes, daring him to come closer. The courtroom gave me a new sense of courage, and I am done with bowing down; if he wants a fight, then I'm ready.

"I bet you wish I was still in jail right now, huh?" he huffs, "sorry to tell ya sis, but you'll never win that battle. No one will ever believe your side of the story again. I'm not making that mistake twice. I'm done looking out for you. In fact, let's go back to how things used to be, before I tried to protect you. Are you ready for that? Cuz I sure am."

Charlie whispers the threats just out of Mom's earshot.

Although I am terrified, I know I have nothing left to lose. Besides the air from my lungs and my beating heart, there is nothing left he can take away. With a roll of my eyes and a deep breath, I spit out the words I've been dying to say for months.

"Charlie, you don't have control over me anymore," I demand, staring him directly in the eye as I raise my shoulders and fix my posture.

Mom gasps from the kitchen as Charlie leaps across the room and places his hands around my neck. Staring directly into my eyes, he tightens his grip and screams out obscenities at me.

"You have no idea what you're doing, you little bitch! I risked everything for you! I wouldn't have had to sleep in jail for two nights, if it wasn't you! Now, I have a criminal record and will never find a job, or a girlfriend, or a life! You appreciate nothing! I hate you! How could you do that to me? You're supposed to have my back, no matter what!"

I struggle for a breath. His eyes turn to sorrow as tears form in the corners.

"I…." my voice trails off. My hearing starts to fade as the room quickly begins to shrink around me. I catch Mom out of the corner of my eye as she turns and walks into the living room. Although I'm in pain, I refuse to cry—refuse to beg. I really destroyed any chance I had at a normal relationship with Charlie, and I'm not sure I'll ever be able to fix it.

Testifying against him didn't change him like I thought it would, in fact, it did the opposite. The room goes black as I fall to the floor. Although I can't see anything, I am still semi-coherent. Charlie's footsteps walk out the door, and moments later the roar of his engine echoes through the house. His tires squeal as he peels out of the driveway, and heads as far away from me as possible.

I grab the rug as I work to replenish the lost air in my lungs. Sitting up, my vision begins to revive and the fogginess in my head clears. Bolting from the house to my truck, I hold myself together just long enough to make it to Bailey's arms.

"Please don't ever make me go back there, please!" I beg of her as I cry uncontrollably on her front porch. The snow melts into my pants as I fall to the ground and yank her jeans begging for a savior.

Bailey squats and takes a seat in the snow, holding me in her arms.

"C'mon Sam, lets go inside," she whispers, lifting me off the wet ground.

As we enter the house, her mom walks through the living room toward me. With outstretched arms, she pulls me to her chest and holds me in her embrace. "Sam, you know if you need a place to stay, you are welcome here," she softly whispers in my ear. "I know you don't have it too easy at home right now."

Her words float through me, helping me to relax. Finally, somewhere I am safe. I've stayed here for several nights a week but moving in was not something I ever saw in the cards. Bailey's parents already had marital issues, and financial problems, the last thing they need is a homeless teenager crashing on their couch and eating their food.

I push a thank-you out through my sobbing, even though I'm not sure I can accept her offer. Although I feel so many different emotions at one time, jealousy tops the list. Bailey is so lucky to live in this house filled with love. I envy her relationship with her mom, a woman so caring and sensitive. As I zone out, wondering how my life would be if I had a mother like that, they concoct a plan to safely get my belongings out of my parents' house.

Apparently, I won't be able to deny her offer.

Staring out the window next to Bailey's bed, I watch as a blue truck slowly drives down the road. I burrow under the blankets, knowing it's only a matter of time until Charlie comes looking for me. Perhaps, one of these days his hands won't release the grip they have on my neck, and I'll be able to slip off into a permanent slumber, finally freeing me from the torture.

Chapter 23

"You can't worry about her, Sam. It's not your job to cater to everyone else's emotions," Bailey tells me as she spikes her hair with gel. "What about you and your feelings?"

I know Bailey is right, but the fear of Mom freaking out when I tell her I'm leaving overcomes my emotions. I have to be clear and set boundaries, without getting into a physical altercation. The only thing I come up with that will keep me safe is to resort to my old standby: writing a letter.

I touch the pen to the paper over and over, but nothing I write sounds genuine. Closing my eyes and pulling in a deep breath, I remember the look on Mom's face all the times she turned away when I needed her the most, and all the times she was supposed to protect me—to stand up for me. Anger and resentment flow out of my heart and down my arm. I open my eyes as the words start to flow from my pen.

Mom,

I'm writing you a letter because telling this to your face would be too difficult. To see you cry or be disappointed would rip my heart out and I cannot do that to you. I love you, Dad, and Charlie so much, but I feel that I need to remove myself from your lives until I can figure out how I feel about the years of pain you have caused me. I hope you can understand. I will be over tomorrow morning to get my stuff.

Love, Sam

It's sentimental, yet straightforward. I am hoping it will instill guilt and sympathy in her, rather than anger. I make sure no one is home before taping it to the front door, and then head back to the safety of Bailey's house for the night.

--

"How many times are you gonna check that thing?" Bailey asks, as she pushes peas around on her dinner plate.

I am anticipating Mom will call me after she reads the letter, but my phone has been silent. She must be making a statement. My stomach twists with ill feelings as I push my plate away, unable to eat.

"Until she responds. Why hasn't she responded? I thought she would be showing up at your door, dragging me out by my hair, demanding I get back home at once. But, nothing? Not a text or a call. This isn't good, Bailey. Not good at all," I worry.

"Maybe she just doesn't care?" Bailey wonders.

"Mom? Not care? I doubt it. The storm is coming. I just don't know when or how. But, it's definitely coming."

After clearing my plate, I retreat to Bailey's room and hide under the covers. Terrified of what the future holds, I lay awake all night, wondering if tomorrow will be my last day on earth. Part of me sincerely hoping I'm right.

--

The morning drive home is short— too short. The birch tree out front has lost a limb, and it sits untouched on the lawn. Pulling around back, I notice Charlie's truck. The driver's window is rolled halfway down, and the morning dew is cleared by the marks of windshield wipers. He's home, and he's awake.

I head inside and see no one. My fingers shake as I place them on the banister and walk up the steps. Quietly pushing open the door to my room, I meander to the bed, glancing around warily. Once there, I place my purse on the beige and black quilt and pull out three garbage bags. Swiftly, I empty each drawer into a bag, while listening cautiously for any noise behind me.

As quickly as I entered, I make my way down the stairs and exit the house of secrets for what I'm hoping is the last time. Throwing the bags in the bed of the truck, I walk around to open my driver's door just in time to see Mom come barreling out of the garage.

"How dare you!" she yells, throwing snow from her boots as she stomps toward me.

The fire I have become so used to seeing in Charlie's eyes has now found a new home in hers. I tremble in fear, unable to say a word as I hurry to open the truck door.

"I'm just getting a few of my things," I say, fumbling with the key. "I'm going to leave now and then you won't have to deal with me anymore."

I hope it's enough to satisfy her as I turn the key and unlatch the door. Lifting the lever, I catch Mom bounding closer out of the corner of my eye. I turn to look at her, just as her fist cracks into my temple.

Momentarily, I'm airborne as I fall to the blacktop; the smell of wet pavement and gasoline are the only things keeping me from passing out. The garage light disappears and reappears as the fists continue to plummet into my head. I can no longer hear well enough to even make sense of the words that are pouring out of her mouth as she climbs on top of me, pinning me down with her legs.

"How could you do this? I gave you everything you could ever want! I was a fantastic mother! Do you know the sacrifices I made for you? You ungrateful little bitch!"

Between the blows, I manage to shield my face with my forearms as I search the background for Dad, wondering why he hasn't come to save me yet.

I catch a glimpse of him through my fingers, standing in the doorway, watching the madness unfold. I know I'm safe now. In a matter of seconds, he will pull her off of me, and I will be able to get out of here.

"Daddy, please help me!" I scream, as I struggle to hold on to consciousness.

I plead with him between every punch, yet he remains silent as he stands completely stationary in the doorway—frozen.

"Daddy, why won't you help me? Please?" I cry through tears of pain, and jolted breaths.

His eyes finally look in my direction, but he doesn't move. I wonder if my voice isn't loud enough. Perhaps, I'm not even speaking at all. Maybe he doesn't hear my pleas. Maybe he's simply a figment of my imagination.

As I look away, Mom's fist connects so hard that my face slams off the concrete.

Why isn't he helping me?

Giving up, I begin to fall into a dark hole as my spirit lifts out of my body and peers down on the events below.

This is it; Mom is going to kill me right here in the driveway. I close my eyes giving in to the pain as the blackness circles around me. Numbness takes over, making the punches almost unnoticeable. I know they are still happening, but I've stopped flinching. I peel my eyes open in one last attempt, and plead with Dad, praying he is right behind her, ready to step in.

"Daddy ... please?" I mouth the words to him, unable to speak.

I'm disappointed to see him still in the same spot, making the same face. In that moment, I realize he isn't going to do anything. I lay my head back down on the pavement and allow my hands to fall to my sides. The screaming begins to meld into mumbling and the heaviness lifts off of me.

Then, it's over.

I move every muscle in my body to make sure they still work, and that I am still alive. Struggling to open my eyes, I roll to my side and vomit on the pavement. Pushing my body off the blacktop, I wipe the tears and try to ignore the throbbing in my head. I know that finally Dad has stepped in and taken Mom aside to settle down. Better late than never.

My vision begins to clear as I see a wave of long black hair, and amber colored eyes.

"Sam, you need to get out of here!" Charlie demands through the darkness. “Now!”

Charlie’s body traps Mom against the siding of the house, as her arms flail behind him. I swallow, and struggle to get to my knees as he flings Mom's arms above her head, and screams in her face to calm her down.

“Get your shit together, Mom!” he yells. “Leave her alone!”

Although my head is pounding, I still realize that Charlie has stepped in once again—when I needed him the most. Guilt soars through my almost limp body. I nod my head and climb into the truck, locking the doors.

My leg shakes as I struggle to push the clutch in and remain conscious long enough to get me to Bailey's house. I stare out the front window as the morning sun shines on Charlie's body still pinning Mom against the wall, and Dad standing off to the side unable to interject. Swerving over the yellow line, I struggle to focus on the road.

My mind fights with my body as it tempts it to pull over and allow me to die. *I will never go back there*. Finally, I manage to coast into Bailey's driveway.

Bailey's mom drops her coffee mug on the table and falls to her knees when I walk through the door. She beckons me to the floor, where she holds me in her arms. I melt into her, shifting in and out of consciousness.

"Bailey, go get a warm washcloth and some blankets; we have to keep her with us," her mom's voice is laced with urgency and concern. I curl my body into her lap as I feel the rag rub softly across my face.

"Should I call an ambulance?" Bailey wonders.

"No," her mom responds. "I'm not putting Sam through testifying against her family again. I'm pretty sure we can treat this here. Let's give it an hour. If she seems to be going downhill, I'll drive her to the emergency room. But, right now, she needs to know she's safe. Get me some warm towels and my first aid kit. She's got this open gash on her forehead I'm going to have to bandage. Grab the pain killers, too. The faster we get them in her, the better she will feel later."

Bailey stares at me, frozen.

"Bailey!" her mom yells. "Get moving! Sam needs you. Don't flake on me!"

I rest my head on her mom's lap. It's throbbing, but I'm able to focus on her mom's face. Tiny hairs stick out of her eyebrows, ready to be plucked, and freckles line the tip of her nose.

"I see you in there, Sam," she whispers. "I'm going to take care of you. Please don't worry. Everything will be ok now."

Knowing I am safe in her arms, I allow my eyes to close while she cares for the wound on my head.

A few hours later, the pounding has faded but Mom's beating is still replaying in my mind. Bailey lifts me off the living room floor and helps me to her bed. She turns out the light and lies next to me, combing her fingers through my hair, attempting to ease my anxiety.

"Bailey, how am I supposed to keep going?" I ask. “What do I do?"

Bailey runs her fingers across my forehead as she quiets me down, refusing to allow me to get worked up again.

"I dunno, Sam, but we will figure it all out together," she whispers. “Now, try to get some rest. You need some sleep, for your body and your mind.”

The throbbing of my eyes begins to settle as Bailey holds the ice pack on them and the pain killers take effect. One final tear runs down my face and soaks into the bedspread, staining the fabric. I begin to fall asleep, praying that I don’t wake up in the morning.

Chapter 24

Bacon sizzles in the pan on the stove. My stomach rumbles as I roll onto my side and search the bedroom for Bailey. Instead, a note scribbled on a tiny piece of stationary situated on an orange bath towel greets me.

Good morning! Go ahead and take a shower and get yourself cleaned up. Mom and I are making you breakfast whenever you're ready.

My head throbs upon standing. When I first opened my eyes, I thought it was all a nightmare—that I never went to Mom's and that none of yesterday's events ever occurred, but my body screams otherwise. Every inch of skin burns. The bones of my face feel broken when my jaw forces a yawn. I quickly retract once the ache begins in my temple, begging me to return to the sheets.

Curling up under the covers and never coming out is insanely inviting. "*I'm just going to pee, then I'll come back,*" I whisper, convincing the bed I'm loyal.

Flicking on the bathroom light, the smell of scented candles and lavender hits me. Several tiny wicks flicker around the tub, and dried spices hang in pantyhose from the ceiling. A fresh bottle of bubble bath and two more towels set on the tubs edge, begging to be used. *A bath can't hurt.* Turning on the spigot, the steam begins to fill the room and hit the spice packs, releasing their heavenly aromas. Bailey has turned this mundane bathroom into my own private spa, and it's exactly what I need.

While the tub fills, I undress. Refusing to look in the mirror before now, I take a deep breath and prepare myself for the gruesome image it's about to cast upon me.

I start at my legs. Spots of blood mix with streaks of dried mud across my jeans. *Way better than I expected.* After a tumble in the washing machine, they should be good as new. *Maybe this isn't as bad as I imagined.* Coasting upwards, my shirt is wrinkled and shifted sideways, which can be blamed on a night of restless sleep. As I adjust it, I notice the neckline is torn and stretched. A splash of blood has dried down the middle, right next to the vomit that I struggled to forget.

Knowing the worst is yet to come, I continue to study my reflection in the mirror. My necklace is twisted, but surprisingly unbroken, and my hair sits knotted in a ball under my left ear. My chin has a little swelling, but it's nothing compared to my enormous purple bottom lip. A gash that has scabbed over runs down the middle. Women pay good money for lips like this—a concept lost by me.

The first tears begin to form in my eyes, preparing to fall. Unsure of whether I want to continue, I stare back down at my shaking hands resting on the bathroom sink.

"Can't get much worse," I mumble.

Tears fall down my cheeks and splash the backs of my hands. Tiny pieces of gravel are stuck inside broken skin on my knuckles. The tears fade and grief takes over. *How could she do this to me? I'm her daughter.*

Coasting around the inside of my mouth with my tongue, open sores taste like cold metal. *My teeth must have cut them.* The bridge of my nose is sliced open, and a blackish-blue color and swelling have made it almost unrecognizable. *Stop now, Sam. You're not going to like what's coming.*

My eyes well up as I shift them to connect with girl in the mirror. *Is that me*? Mountains of black-and-blue stare back at me. Broken blood vessels speckle my cheeks and forehead. A make-shift bandage covers an injury on my temple where the tape has started to peel. Blood has soaked through the gauze. Peeling back what's left, an open gash becomes apparent. The bandage takes the semi-formed scab with it, and blood trickles down to my eyebrow. I grab a washcloth and shove it on the wound, attempting to control the bleeding. I stare in the mirror one last time and notice the whites surrounding my emerald irises are solid red, like some sort of Christmas decoration.

I look away, unable to stare at the horrific image any longer. Turning my back to the mirror, I pull a pair of scissors out of Bailey's bathroom drawer. After undressing, and throwing my clothes in the hamper, I slip into the burning water. Hovering the blade over my left wrist, I wonder how long it would take to die this way. *Will it be painful? Will I pass out first? Should I slit both wrists, or will one suffice?* Just as I touch the metal blade to my skin, there is a knock on the door.

"Sam, are you coming out soon?" Bailey's voice whispers through the crack in the door, "I made home fries ... I know they are your favorite!"

I refuse to answer. Staring at the silver blade, I push it on my skin just hard enough to draw blood. A single drop exits my vein and falls into the water below, causing ripples to soar across the surface. The tiny, blood-stained waves hit me in the thigh and it snaps me back to reality.

My goal in all of this was to stop the abuse; to get out of the circle of hell and start a new life. *How is killing myself going to prove anything?* It wouldn't change how they treated me, or how they treat anyone else. The only people it would hurt are the ones who have struggled to help me through.

Charlie saved my life last night. Although it's completely abnormal, he's trying to prove that he gives a shit about me. *What if we can work on this together? What if there's hope for us in the future?*

I close the blades and toss the scissors onto the floor. Grabbing the washcloth off my head, I wrap it around my wrist to stop the bleeding as I enjoy the serenity of a good soak. Bailey would be destroyed if she opened the door and found me drowning in a sea of red. It wouldn't have stopped me, but I can't validate ruining her life just because of the rubble mine has become. It's not my time to go, at least not yet.

I step out of the tub and dry off before Bailey's attempt at a homemade breakfast gets cold. My sweater covers my bruised ribcage but there is no chance of hiding my face. Bailey's parents' jaws drop when I walk into the dining room. They both stand up from their chairs and walk toward me with their arms elongated. I fall into them as they hold me for the longest embrace I've felt in years.

Her mom kisses my head and checks my wound. "Please, Sam, come join us for breakfast," she directs.

I smile at Bailey as she spoons home fries onto my plate and sprinkles them with salt and pepper. Two pain killers sit on my napkin, and her mom applies a new bandage to my head as I munch on a piece of sausage. This is the closest I've ever come to having a real family, and I'm so incredibly thankful that I found Bailey. Hopefully, she can help me figure out a way to move forward, with or without Charlie in my life. The past is now just that, and I have my whole future to look forward to. And, for a moment, after the worst night of my life, I am happy.

Chapter 25

"What about this one? Two-bedroom, one bath, with a pond," Bailey asks as she shoves the newspaper in my face. I take a puff of my cigarette before I grab it out of her hand and blow circles of smoke around it.

"Uh, $1,100 a month?" I say, giggling at Bailey before tossing the paper back in her lap. "I'm a bartender, not a millionaire."

Bailey continues to peruse the classifieds as I stare at her and smile. A few weeks ago, I managed to scoop up a job as a bartender at a restaurant a few towns over. The boss offered to train me for free, mainly because I was 'young and cute'. I have to wear low-cut shirts and tight pants, and the scene is rough on the weekends, but the money is killer. Even though Bailey sits breezing through apartment listings with me, I know she doesn't want me to leave.

"Here's one, Sam; studio apartment with everything included—$550 a month!" she exclaims as she pushes my shoulder and leans in front of me. "It's even right down the road from your work."

I read the listing a few times before I decide to call the number.

"You can come by later today, if you want. I'm home all day," the woman on the other end states. "You'll need first month's rent and a security deposit of five hundred. Don't waste my time if you don't have the money."

"I got the money," I state. "When is it available?"

"Right away. You can move in today if you want," she responds.

"Ok, I'll see you in about an hour."

--

Awkward silence fills the car on the ride there. I know Bailey is sad, but I have long overstayed my welcome at her parents' house. We pull into a cul-de-sac and raise our heads to follow the immense house in front of us.

"Number 203," Bailey reads the address of the notepad I had written it on earlier. "This is the place."

I fold my directions as I park the truck, and we both step out. Immediately, I regret my decision to wear jeans and a ripped sweatshirt as I lift my hand to ring the doorbell—wardrobe choices never were one of my strong suits. A middle-aged, dark-haired woman flings open the door. Her arm is hooked around a mixing bowl, and flour covers her apron. A toddler hangs on her leg while she attempts to shake him off.

"You must be Sam," she says, as she wipes the hair from her face with the back of her hand. "Just hang on a second, I'll send my husband out to show you the apartment. I'm in the middle of sixty different things," she laughs.

I smile and nod as I back onto the porch and watch her walk into the kitchen. She sits down at the table with her two sons, each taking turns adding ingredients to the bowl.

Bailey and I gaze around at the pristine landscaping and expensive vehicles that line the driveways of all the houses on the block.

"Hi girls, I'm Mark," an older, gray-haired man appears from behind the side of the house. "Your apartment is out back. You can follow me."

My Apartment.

An uncontrollable smile stretches across my finally healed face when I hear those words. I take a deep breath and follow him down the driveway and around back. The steps to the front door are rickety, and widely spaced. I feel like an antelope climbing them. Turning around, I giggle at Bailey as she struggles and grips the railing for support.

I have a porch. I've always wanted a porch.

Standing there for a moment as Mark opens the door, I glance at the backyard. A large in-ground pool sits empty, a single tube being pushed by the wind is the only movement. Birds peck at apples that litter the ground under the trees in the orchard, and a squirrel climbs over chicken wire that's surrounding a family garden.

"Ok, Sam," Mark says, "you and your friend go ahead in and look around. If you have any questions, I'll be right out here. I have a few things to do in the yard."

I blink several times before stepping into the apartment; I want to be absolutely positive this isn't a dream. Staring down at my sneakers as they scuff onto the linoleum floor, I stand in the middle of a small—but quaint—kitchen. The refrigerator hums an inviting tune as I study the sink, stove and countertop. White cabinets line the entire apartment. Plenty of storage, considering I only have three garbage bags worth of belongings.

"I'll need pots and pans. Dishes. Curtains. Lamps. A bed," I ramble. "Bailey, where am I gonna get all this stuff?" I ask.

"Sam, I'm sure we have something you can borrow until you have the money to buy your own furniture. Don't worry about that right now. Just see if you like the place, first."

I continue walking until my feet feel the soft, navy carpet below them.

"Uh, Sam," Bailey whispers, "is this the whole thing?"

I chuckle under my breath at Bailey's comment. She extends both of her arms, pretending to touch each wall, and then circles the room. “It’s like the size of my bedroom.”

"That's what a studio apartment is, Bailey," I tell her confidently, slightly offended by her mocking. "Basically, its just one big room that’s separated into sections."

I glance around, decorating the space in my head.

“Just think of how fun it will be to search for cool stuff at auctions and yard sales with me, Bailey.”

A look of uncertainty fills her questioning face. “Whatever you say, Sam. As long as you’re happy, I guess it’s ok with me. You know, you could just stay with us a little longer. Maybe check out some more places?”

I shake my head, “I’m so glad I got to stay with you, Bailey, but I think it’s time I move forward. Maybe once you graduate, we can get a place together.”

After exiting the apartment, I sign the lease with Mark's pen as I trade him my savings account for the keys. They jingle as they fall into my hand—the ring of freedom.

Chapter 26

The months fly by as the sweet warmth of summer gives way to crisp, fall hues. It's hard to believe it's been almost a year since I've seen or talked to my family. I sit quietly, alone on my futon reading a book, as I listen to the soothing sound of the kitchen faucet dripping water onto the dirty dishes in the sink.

As I stand and walk toward the door, my phone buzzes on the kitchen counter. Always secretly hoping it is Mom or Charlie calling to apologize and mend our broken relationship, I am disappointed when Bailey's name scrolls across the screen. I decide to ignore it as I pull a cigarette out of the pack and light it up on my way out the door.

The porch railing creaks when I lean my weight on it and stare up at the stars above me. Every night I sit out here, smoking a cigarette, wondering if they miss me. *Do they ever question where I am or how I am doing?* I always put my cigarette out and head inside before I allow myself to fall victim to regret.

--

The sun breaks through the icy morning air when my phone falls off the table and onto the floor, obnoxiously vibrating. It is way too early for work to be calling. I wipe my eyes and slip on my glasses. Shock engulfs me as I read the white letters.

Mom.

It is the call I have been waiting almost a year to receive, and I am somehow still completely unprepared. Before allowing myself to ignore it, I hit the answer button and raise the phone to my ear. My words are lost in the sound of Mom's trembling voice.

"Sam ... is that you?" she asks, quietly.

I have longed to hear her voice. Time hasn't healed the injuries she's caused in me, but it has helped calm the anger. I rest my arms on my legs so they stop shaking as I muster up the strength to say something.

"Yeah, Ma; it's me."

I can hear her sigh from the other end as she fights to keep herself from crying. Her voice is so shaky that I'm finding it hard to recognize. She works on simultaneous deep breaths to push down the hysterics I hear creeping up.

"Sam, your brother is in jail," she cries. "They came and got him two weeks ago."

I fall backwards on my bed and stare at the ceiling in silence. The sensation of my heart banging on my spine is the only proof that this is not a figment of my imagination.

"He asked me to call you because he wants to see you," she says, as her voice begins to settle. "He's at the county jail on Broad Street. Visiting hours are ‘til 5."

Without a farewell, the phone clicks off. I run Mom's words over and over in my head, making sure I heard her right.

What could Charlie possibly have done this time to land him in jail, and why the hell does he want to see me?

Chapter 27

That afternoon, I find myself parked at the county jail, staring at the steel doors for 30 minutes before pulling my keys and walking in.

The building is ice cold. The door slams behind me as I trudge toward the security counter. After filling out paperwork, and signing papers I don't bother to read, I hop through a metal detector. The red alarm sounds, and I'm quickly directed to a female guard who frisks me—leaving no inch untouched. She confiscates my metal-studded belt and small knife I keep on my hip, tossing it into a plastic bin.

"You can get these things when you're finished," she demands. "You have anything else on you that is on the list?" she asks, pointing to a piece of paper hanging on the wall behind her.

I scan over the list of items and shake my head, "No."

"Have a seat. I'll take you back in a few minutes," she mumbles behind furrowed brows.

No wonder cops get such a bad rep. Maybe you should try to be a little kinder to those on the outside. Just because I have a brother in jail, doesn't mean I did anything to deserve being treated like a criminal.

"Let's go, Samantha," she states as she waves her ID in front of the sensor and opens the door to the visiting room.

I follow her closely, hurrying my pace to match hers.

"You sit here, hun," she says as she points to a small table. "We will bring your brother in shortly. Officer Snarp will read you the rules while you wait."

An old man with no more than three hairs on his head begins to explain the rules of our visit. His condescending tone aggravates me. *What is with these people?*

I vaguely listen as I look around at the other families in the room.

A young woman with a baby hung on her shoulder sits at the table next to me, shaking uncontrollably, as a man in an orange jumpsuit walks through the doors. She glares in his eyes as he starts to cry.

"Is this my little angel?" he asks.

She smiles at him and nods her head, tears streaming down her face.

The door handle twists, catching my attention. I focus on it, freezing when Charlie's figure emerges from the shadows. Once he locks eyes with me, he doesn't draw back. Taking a seat, he places his hands on the table. I cock my head to the side and study his body language. His clenched fists begin to relax and lay flat in front of him as his hard face begins to soften. I try to act tough as I fight the tears that are begging to escape. Nothing could've prepared me for seeing him in here—my big brother.

"Hey, Sam," he says, softly.

I blink at him to let him know that I am in here somewhere—that I'm not just a wax figure sitting in this cold-metal chair.

"I guess Mom called you," he adds, fumbling with his fingers. "I'm glad you're here; I have something I want to tell you."

My mind races as ideas uncontrollably bounce around my head. There are thousands, no millions, of things Charlie could want to say. Maybe he will tell the officer about that night with Mom or apologize for putting me in the middle of the Colleen situation. Perhaps he is going to ask for forgiveness for hurting me all those times he lost his temper when we were kids. Maybe he can somehow erase the last 18 years and replace them with happy memories and get us out of this place. Whatever it is, I am more than ready to hear it. I take a deep breath as I fold my hand on my lap and wait; my eyes scrunch as they continue to fight against crying.

"Sam, I got arrested a few weeks ago for domestic abuse against my girlfriend," he begins. "Considering it was my second offense, the court decided I needed to spend some time in jail."

Good. A small smile spreads across my face, knowing Charlie is finally getting punished for his actions.

"I've been seeing a therapist daily for the last two weeks, and she helped me realize some things," he adds.

I pinch my leg as I listen, hoping it will wake me up from this dream. I wince away from the pain.

"She says part of my therapy is apologizing to all the people I've wronged. She says we can't progress until I show remorse for my past actions," he says, refusing to lock eyes with me.

I sigh at the attitude he has toward the statement but try to support him.

"Sam, I cannot change what I did to you, or how I treated you. I don't regret standing up for you at the party or trying to get back at Colleen for hurting you the way she did," he says, giving me an opening to interject.

I remain silent, hoping this isn't the end of his half-hearted admission of guilt. When I don't give him an easy exit from his apology, anger flashes in his eyes, and he lowers his voice so only I can hear him.

"Listen, they aren't going to let me out of here if I'm not showing any progress," he tells me as he sits back and rests his hands on his lap. "We both know I don't belong in here, Sam."

Tears of anger and disappointment begin to flow down my face as I struggle to keep my composure, unwilling to allow Charlie to see my weakness. All heads in the room turn to me as I wipe my eyes on my sleeve.

A wave of frustration rolls through my head as I realize Charlie is nowhere near ready to change. Afraid that years of resentment will begin to plummet from my mouth if I don't leave immediately, I push the chair back and motion to the guard that we are finished.

Silent tears roll down my cheek as I whisper, "Goodbye, Charlie," to him and the guards escort him away, back to his temporary home for the next 11 months.

"Goodbye, sis," he says, turning his head around his shoulder. "I wish I knew what to say to fix this, but I just don't. I hope you can eventually forgive me."

I clench my jaw and offer him a tiny wave, hoping he knows the internal battle I'm losing. He turns back around and is lost through the white metal door. I look down at the teardrops that have fallen on the fading varnish of the table and wipe the moisture with my sleeve. With a sense of disappointment, I grab my belongings and exit the building, taking a huge gulp of fresh air. Swallowing a lump of guilt, I leave Charlie behind, right where he belongs.

Chapter 28

Hours pass before I have the strength to drive. Several times I open the truck door and walk back toward the jail entrance. *I need to save him like he saved me. I owe him that.* The ring of my cellphone stops me halfway across the parking lot.

"Did you see him?" Bailey asks.

"Yeah," I respond, defeated. "He hasn't made an effort to change yet. I know he's deep in there somewhere, but he's buried behind so much anger and betrayal, that I can't get to him."

"I'm so sorry, Sam. Just give it time. He's getting the help he needs. Hopefully one day he will come around, and you guys can have the relationship you did when you were kids."

"Yeah," I push through tears. "Hopefully."

The roads are familiar as I coast down them—I know exactly where they are leading me. Pulling over on the edge of the woods, the sun begins to fall in the west casting shadows through the yellow hue. The leaves rustle under my feet as I make my way to the destination.

Pushing limbs from my path and ducking under spider webs, I search for the clearing, letting my heart lead the way. The trees begin to open as my feet halt at the edge of the water. Although overrun with lily pads and horsetails as tall as me, it's exactly how I remember it; the one place that isn't littered with painful memories. An oak tree has fallen on the far side, and a blue-jay sits on its splintered wood, staring at me—welcoming me home.

A smile draws across my face, as a calmness sweeps through my body.

I circle the edge of the pond looking for our bench. It still exists; buried underneath a small fallen pine with mushrooms sprouting around its base. I push the tree aside and brush off the dead leaves before taking a seat. Moisture from the rotting log quickly soaks my jeans from below, but I don't care.

Stretching my feet in front of me, my sneakers come to rest at the edge of the blue-green water. The branches dance in the wind above me, as the shadows begin to fade and the first stars of the night pierce through the blackened sky.

I close my eyes as I listen to the noise of the woods allowing the fear to release. A bullfrog bellows to my left, and mosquitos threaten to bite my uncovered skin. A lonely owl howls in the background as the crickets begin to play their symphony of music. After all these years, the magic of this place still exists—forever protected by its innocence. It is the one place that Charlie will forever remain immortal to me and—for now—the only place I can trust him.

An hour passes. Rustling in the woods starts to worry me, so I stand and brush the leaves that cling to my legs, breathing the pond in one final time. Turning toward the truck, I stop to pick up a rock that stands stationary in my path. Tossing it over my shoulder, I hear it plop into the water and turn around to see the ripples scurry across the surface, reminding me of my attempts to save Charlie. The rock sinks to the bottom, where it will lay forever, undisturbed in the darkness.

Continuing my steps toward the truck, I catch something out of the corner of my eye. Fishing wire climbs to the sky from the forest floor, twisted and knotted, catching the first light from the moon. Moving in, I examine it closer. With a firm tug, a worn stick follows the string from beneath the leaves where it's attached to the base. I can't believe it. Although broken and tattered, it's exactly how I remember—just as perfect as the day Charlie created it.

I pull a sheet from the back seat and fold the relic for safe keeping. Tucking it down on the floor of the truck, it bumps the wooden memory box I grabbed from my bedroom the night I moved out. As much as I want to cry, the tears don't seem to come as I emerge from the body of water that brought me so much joy as a young girl.

Leaving Charlie's soul in the darkness behind me, I hope that one day he will be able to find his way out. The yellow line fades as I travel back to my childhood, for just a moment to say goodbye.

I whisper in the darkness, "I forgive you," as fogginess fills my head.

Maybe one day he will come find me, and beg for my forgiveness, but I'm not holding my breath.

Epilogue

The driveway is broken. Tiny plants and weeds have taken over the cracks, turning what used to be a flat pavement, into a crumbled mess. The garage door is rotted, and ivy vines have grown up the molding and across the windowsill.

"I can't believe it's been ten years since I've been here," I whisper.

"You sure you want to do this?" Jake asks from the passenger seat. "You've made so much progress. Will going in there destroy all of that?"

Twisting the wedding band on my finger, my heart begins to race. "So many memories and secrets hide behind those walls, what if I can't handle it? What if I fall back into that girl I used to be?"

Jake grabs my hand; the sweat from my palm drenches his immediately.

"Sam, you are NOT that girl anymore. You've dealt with all of that. You are so much stronger now. Look how far we have come. Ten years ago, you thought you would never be able to forgive me, but we worked through it. Anything is possible. You need to at least try."

My stomach bumps the steering wheel as I reach to shut off the ignition. "The stress of all of this cannot be good for the baby," I whine.

"We can always leave and go home, Sam. If that's what you want."

Glancing at the garage door, I catch a glimpse of the upstairs curtain as it blows in the wind. Behind it, a man stares through the glass.

"Charlie?"

"Where?" Jake asks. "Did you know he was going to be here?"

"No," I respond. "He didn't say anything about it at our last therapy session. He said he didn't need the closure—that seeing *her* again would just cause him to take too many steps back. He's come so far, too. We are finally at a healthy place. The timing of all this is just... horrible. But that's Mom for ya. Always having to control everything and everyone."

The back door swings open, and Charlie waves to us. "You guys gonna sit in the truck all day? You afraid to come in, Sam? It'll be alright. I got you."

Forcing myself from the safety of the car, I follow Charlie inside. The screen door crashes behind me when I forget to ease it closed. Startled from the noise, my heart bangs against my ribcage and my lungs struggle to inflate. Jake makes small talk with Charlie while we wander through the darkened house. The scent of Mom's perfume has seeped into every empty room, and it stirs up all the bittersweet memories I've ever had in this place. The carpet on the back porch is exactly how it was ten years ago. The same chairs sit in only a slightly different position, and pictures of Charlie and I still hang from the mantle above the fireplace. *It's like I never left.*

The kitchen is empty. The only noise is the constant low buzz of the refrigerator, void of any pictures or magnets that used to litter the outside. I can imagine Mom in her apron, pushing blonde strands of hair from her eyes as she struggles to cook while scolding us to stay out of her way. So many family dinners I was forced to endure; dinners I attended, but never enjoyed. An inch of dust covers the dining room table—a dumping ground for the junk mail Dad retrieves from the box but doesn't know how to sort. One chair, mine, sits to the side, broken.

"Are you ready, Sam?" Charlie asks, concerned. "She's in the living room."

Uncontrollable shaking takes over as I struggle to prepare myself. It's been over a decade since I've seen my mother, and I'm not sure exactly what to expect. There are so many things I need to hear to get the closure I so desperately seek, but I know I'm probably not going to get any of them.

"Remember what the therapist said, Sam," Charlie whispers. "It's closure for you—not for her."

I nod, thankful that he's here.

Jake takes a seat at the kitchen table, sorting through the mail, keeping his distance. "I'll give you guys some time. If you need me, I'll be right here."

Taking my hand, Charlie leads me through the doorway and into the living room. The vibration of the oxygen machine creates a sort of white noise in the background. The walls begin closing in when I see her, staring out the window, lying motionless in bed. Her blonde locks are sliced down to gray fuzz. A scarf covers most of her head, except for the top where tiny strands sneak out, catching the suns' rays. Her once perfectly toned skin now holds a ghostly tone, and bags have formed under her beautiful blue eyes.

Once she hears our footsteps, she turns. "Samantha," she whispers through the room. "It's about time you came back."

Mixed emotions flood my core. I so desperately want to crawl on her lap and fall into her arms. I want her to hold me, and kiss me, and tell me everything will be ok. I want her to miraculously turn into the mother I needed her to be all these years in the blink of an eye.

"Come, sit down," she instructs. "I have something for you."

I do as she says and take a seat on the leather sofa at her feet. My heart battles with my head, desperately wanting to run to her, but knowing I'll be rejected as soon as I get too close.

"Your father hired a nursing staff to sit with me. They keep telling me I've got time yet, but I'm not so sure. I think it's sooner than later."

Unsure of what to say, I stare down at my stomach that is now shifting around with large movements.

"It's a shame I won't get to meet her," she says, pointing to my belly.

Who says you would've gotten to meet her, anyway?

"Yeah," I push out, knowing there wasn't a snowball's chance in hell that I was going to let her ruin my daughter's life too.

"Hard to believe you and Charlie are in the same room. Surprised you two can get along long enough. Guess you both are excited that you'll be rid of me soon. All your problems will disappear."

If only it was that easy.

I swat at a bug that lands on my knee. "You said you had something for me?" I ask, ignoring her previous quips.

Mom points toward her office, instructing Charlie to retrieve a box from the corner.

"When I die," she begins. "The house will be sold. Your father will get most of the money, and the rest will go into a savings account for any future grandkids, including that one," she explains, pointing to my uterus. "There are two boxes in the office of some personal belongings I picked up around the house. Some things are my parents' that I'm passing along to you guys. Do with them what you wish."

Following Charlie into the office, I stare at the small cardboard box in the corner, hardly big enough to fit a pair of boots.

“This is all we get?” I whisper, just out of Mom’s earshot.

“Yeah. Did you want anything else, anyway? It’s not like we built good memories in this house, Sam. Everything can go in the dumpster, for all I care,” Charlie declares.

I know he’s right, but parting with these memories—as painful as they are—is still difficult. I only got one childhood, and I’m desperately clinging to it.

I join Mom back in the living room, refusing to sit.

“Is there something you came for, Sam?” she asks.

Tears fall down my face when I can’t hold them back any longer. “Why was I so unlovable?” I cry. “What did I do wrong? You hate me! How do you hate your own daughter—your own flesh and blood? You carried me inside of you; your blood ran through my veins. You sat in labor for 3 days and raised me. How can you sit here, right in front of me, with absolutely nothing to say?”

“Sam,” Charlie says sternly, grabbing my shoulders. “I think it’s time to go.”

“No!” I yell, throwing his arms away. “I need to know the answer!”

“It’s not going to be what you want to hear,” he whispers. “She’s not going to give you what you need.”

“You’re dying!” I scream. “You are dying and you can’t even tell me you love me! You would rather go out of this world holding onto your pride, than holding on to your family. I will never forgive you for that!”

Before she can answer, I sprint from the room. Jake rushes behind me, catching my body before it collapses in the yard outside.

“Are you ok, Sam?” he asks.

I blubber in his arms, "She never loved me. Why didn't she love me? How can you not love your own daughter?"

Without a word, Jake lifts me out of the grass and sets me on the bench outside the back door. A truck pulls in the driveway and a young woman exits.

"That's the nurse," Charlie explains as he meanders through the screen door. "She's going to help Mom shower and get cleaned up."

Knowing I got everything I'm going to get from Mom, I brush the grass clippings from my pants and stand.

Charlie grabs my hand, "Come with me for a minute. Do you mind, Jake?"

Jake questionably shakes his head, "I don't mind, as long as you take care of her, Charlie."

"With my life," Charlie responds.

Pulling me behind him, Charlie heads down the hill and through the woods. Helping me over fallen logs and through broken limbs, the pond is barely visible. What used to stretch a quarter mile wide, and six feet deep has been diminished to a small puddle of water, five feet wide.

"What happened to it?" I wonder.

"Nature took it back," Charlie responds. "Time changes so many things, Sam. Even things that seem invincible."

Glancing along the water's edge, I search for our bench, but the tree it was carved from has rotted away, leaving only a memory in its place.

"Our childhood was awful, Sam. We had two really bad parents, and right now we are losing one of them. She's never going to tell you the words you need to hear, because she can't. We lost Mom so many years ago, and we never got her back. She loves you, Sam, but not in the way you need. She loves you the only way she is capable. It's all she can give. You either need to accept that and move forward, or you will be stuck in this place for the rest of your life," Charlie explains as he throws a rock into the water.

"What if I can't?" I ask.

"If you can't? Then you'll be no better than her. Mom is so angry from her childhood and all the things that she grew up dealing with. She never found a release from them, and it ate her alive. Instead of stopping the cycle of abuse, she kept it going by pushing it on us. If you don't find an outlet for the anger from our childhood, it will destroy the life of that little girl you're bringing into this world."

I fall to the forest floor, sitting on leaves that used to rest on the bottom of our pond.

I know he's right, as hard as it is to hear. If I don't find a way to stop the cycle, I'll ruin my daughter's life. Anger has destroyed so much of me, and I can't let it destroy her. I need her to know I love her from the moment she enters this world, and every single day until I take my last breath. Hopefully, it's a realistic goal.

"Charlie?" I wonder. "Do you love me?"

Charlie takes a seat next to me on the leaves and wraps his arm around my shoulder. "More than anything else in the world."

Jake yells from the porch, "Charlie, the nurse needs to know where the shampoo is. You better get up here!"

Charlie's amber eyes are soft. In the course of almost 30 years, we've come full circle. I'm blessed to have a brother like Charlie, and for the first time, I realize he's blessed to have a sister like me.

--

The phone rings two days later, and Charlie's voice holds a somber tone.

"Mom didn't make it through the night," he says. "Dad called around 5:00. I guess her heart gave out."

My breathing becomes shallow. I need to cry but am unable to. I figured tears would stream down my face when this moment came; that I would be unable to catch my breath and swallow my spit; that all the years of guilt would come rushing out. However, I'm surprisingly calm.

"Ok, Charlie. Just let me know what's next," I respond. "I'll talk to you later."

Before I hang up the phone, Charlie yells through the other end.

"Sam, wait!"

Lifting the phone back to my ear, I wonder what Charlie wants to say.

"The box that Mom left for you… do you want me to bring it over?"

"Sure," I respond. "There's no rush, really. I can't imagine it's anything important, anyway."

--

The brown cardboard box sits on my dining room table for two days before I have the strength to look inside. Peeling off the lid, I blow the dust into the air. Pictures of us as kids are neatly situated in albums, dated and filed for every year of our lives. Family vacations where Dad wore a green and yellow swimsuit, and Charlie went scuba diving in the Bahamas along with birthdays and Christmas mornings. Distant memories so carefully protected—so perfectly preserved.

Underneath the albums is a pair of tiny ballet shoes, with the name 'Samantha Mallon' written along the sole. A medal from my first dance recital is folded neatly inside the toe. My baby book, completely filled out, causes tears to roll down my cheek as I run my fingers over Mom's handwriting, knowing I will never see it again. The smell of her perfume coats the entire contents, and I pray that it never disappears.

Digging to the bottom, a black notebook hits my fingers. I've seen it before. It's the same notebook that sat on Mom's dresser after she got out of the hospital, the one that held all her secrets that we were never allowed to touch.

Is it in here by mistake? There's no way she meant to give this to me.

Opening the first page, I'm hit with a post-it note fastened to the paper.

Dear Sam,

I hope this answers all of your questions, because I know you have so many.

Taking a seat on the chair, I continue, barely able to see through the rivers of tears exiting my eyes.

Even though I could never say it out loud, I do love you, Samantha. Always have—always will. Please forgive me.

I slam the notebook shut, throwing it back into the box. Years of anger rise to the surface, and I fling the box off of the table, littering the floor with its contents.

Dad enters the room, just as I struggle to get it together.

"What are you doing here?" I yell. "Get out!"

Before I can say another word, Dad wraps me in his arms. "Sam, please. I know how hard this is for you."

It's the first time my father has ever hugged me. His arms pull me in, and the tiny hairs of his beard press into my forehead. My body is tense and rigid, unwilling to fall into the embrace. *Why now?*

"No!" I yell, pushing him away. "Where were you ten years ago in the parking lot when Mom beat me up? You just watched! Where were you when I was a kid and Charlie gave me black eyes every other week? Do you know anything about me? Do you even give a rat's ass about me? It's too late! You can't just walk in here and hug me and expect that everything is going to be ok. You spent almost 30 years screwing up my life! You and Mom! I can't just forget that!"

Taken aback by my tone, Dad begins to walk away. "I just wanted to make sure you were alright. I understand you lost your mother, Sam, but I lost my wife of 40 years, too."

Guilt immediately hits me. "I'm sorry, Dad. I understand that, but I don't think I can swallow my pride and be there for you when you were never there for me. I've spent years dealing with a lot of crap, and I'm not going to let you erase that with a hug."

With a nod, Dad leaves the room and heads back to his car to leave.

"Wait," I yell, jogging to catch up. "Can I ask you one thing?"

He turns on his heels. "Anything, Sam."

"Do you think I was the reason Mom went to the institution?"

Shifting his eyes from the ground to mine, his face turns somber. "Your mother loved you more than anything in this world, Sam. Read the notebook from the hospital, it'll explain everything. She had so many horrible things happened to her—things she had blocked out until after you were born. It was just bad timing. It wasn't you, Samantha. You were the reason she got out of the hospital. You saved her. I hope you believe that. Call me if you need anything else."

I kick a stone in my path as I head back into the house, unsure of everything.

"Sam," Dad yells from the car.

I turn as he pulls up beside me.

"If it's any consolation, I love you. Maybe not how you need or want, but I do and I always will. You are my daughter, and that will never change."

Tears well in my eyes, but I walk away before they fall. I don't want him to know how easy it is to break me. Running up the steps and into the bedroom, I grab the black notebook off the floor. Opening to the first page, I begin to read the cursive handwriting that's been hiding for more than 20 years.

November 3rd,

My daughter's birthday is today. It's the first time I'll miss her birthday since I brought her into this world. It must be so disappointing to know your mother is in an institution. What kind of life is that for a little child? I wish I could figure out how to get home to her and how to explain this all, but I don't have any idea where to even begin. If I could just hold her in my arms and tell her I love her every single day for the rest of my life, then I would consider it ok. I pray my daughter knows I love her when I'm not there to tell her and that one day, she will understand that I did this all for her. That I tried, and that even if I fail, and she gives up on me, my love will never die.

I close the notebook and set it on the bed next to me. Staring out the window, I notice a large black butterfly landing on the tree branch a foot away. Its tiny wings flap in slow motion, warming in the mid-day sun. A sudden pop in my stomach changes my attention. A warm wet liquid soaks my pants and the comforter.

"Jake!" I yell. "I think my water just broke."

He rushes up the steps and into the bedroom, dialing the OBGYN on his way.

“Are you ready for this?” he asks.

I nod my head, “Yes, I *finally* have everything I need.”

About The Author

C. L. Heckman, a small-town writer from Pennsylvania, grew up with a love of words but was never sure exactly how to put them to use. She dabbled in poetry and song writing as a teenager but spent the majority of her time on the back of her Arabian horses, showing all over the country at regional and national levels.

After graduating high school, she attended a university, where she studied for her BA in psychology, before needing to take time off to care for her ailing father. She decided that college was not in the cards for the time being and became a full-time bartender, and part-time riding instructor for many years.

Years later, after having her oldest daughter, she decided to pursue her writing goals and wrote Charlie's Secret on the wordpad app of her IPhone in just a few weeks.

Charlie's Secret is inspired by Heckman's own memories that she revisited while in years of cognitive therapy for anxiety, depression and PTSD, but written in a fictional narrative. The story is personal, and heartbreaking, and she almost didn't publish it. She states how terrifying it was to open your heart and soul to the world and have them judge every single aspect of you as a person.

However, since the publishing, Heckman has had some amazing opportunities to share the book with other victims and offer support to them during their own individual journeys. Charlie's Secret has recently been added to several colleges across the US as required reading.

After the incredibly positive response to Charlie's Secret, Heckman has published a sequel to the story titled, Sam's Truth. In 2022, she will be writing the final installment to the series with hopes of publishing it by summer 2023.

She spends most of her time outdoors with her two daughters, riding their five horses on their small farm. She loves to hear from readers and fans. Please feel free to contact her at the below options.

"C. L. Heckman- Author" page on Facebook
@cl_heckman on tiktok
Charliespond@hotmail.com